The
Young Oxford Book
— of —
Supernatural Stories

The
Young Oxford Book
of
Supernatural Stories

DENNIS PEPPER

OXFORD UNIVERSITY PRESS
Oxford • New York • Toronto

Oxford University Press, Great Clarendon Street, Oxford OX2 6DP
Oxford New York
Athens Auckland Bangkok Bogota
Buenos Aires Calcutta Cape Town Chennai Dar es Salaam Delhi
Florence Hong Kong Istanbul Karachi Kuala Lumpur Madrid
Melbourne Mexico City Mumbai Nairobi Paris Sao Paulo
Singapore Taipei Tokyo Toronto Warsaw
and associated companies in
Berlin Ibadan

Oxford is a trade mark of Oxford University Press

This selection and arrangement © Dennis Pepper 1996
First published 1996
First published in paperback 1998

A CIP catalogue record for this book is available
from the British Library

ISBN 0 19 278146 4 (hardback)
ISBN 0 19 278157 X (paperback)

Printed and bound in Great Britain by
Biddles Ltd, Guildford and King's Lynn
Typeset in Stempel Garamond
by Sue Singleton, Oxford
Cover photograph by Rob Judges

Contents

Introduction

Although ghosts are supernatural beings, not all supernatural stories are about ghosts. Many are about creatures or entities that, whatever they are, cannot be thought of as ghosts and deal with events and happenings that are certainly super-natural but are not necessarily ghostly. This is a collection of 'non-ghost' supernatural stories. If you prefer the ghostly kind you should read *The Young Oxford Book of Ghost Stories*.

If the occasional ghost does creep in (and I'm sure it does) it is because I cannot always make up my mind whether a particular story involves a ghost or not. Is there a *ghost* in John Gordon's 'Bewitched' or Dennis Hamley's 'Dog on Board'? Then there are *poltergeists*, those rackety household 'ghosts' that harass people with noises and by throwing things and generally creating mayhem until eventually they drive their unfortunate victims away. There is plenty of poltergeist-like activity in Terry Tapp's 'The Junk Room' but we don't know whether this is the work of a poltergeist or some other malevolent manifestation. It *may* be a poltergeist—but then I'm not at all sure that poltergeists should be thought of as 'ghosts' at all. However, ghosts or non-ghosts where I found a good story I put any doubts I had to one side and included it.

Most of the stories do not involve ghosts or anything like them. Instead you will find werewolves and vampires, witches of various kinds, the re-animated dead (and Death herself in the form of a beautiful woman). You will find the Banshee, a Water Mamma, La Diablesse, and even an angel. But you will also find things you cannot put a name to. What is happening in the houses (there are two or three of them) that reject people? Or the wood that nearly kills a man intent on cutting it down? Bridgey is protected by the Grimblett, who comes to her rescue when Uncle Sully threatens to 'throttle the life from her', but there is no one to protect Nigel from Hacky Basham's glass eye or ferrety-faced Joe Larkin from retribution for his crime against the dead. Innocent like Nigel or like Joe Larkin guilty, if you tangle with the supernatural (or if the supernatural tangles with you) you are likely to have a nasty time of it.

In the *Ghost Stories* collection I brought together writers whose work is mainly intended for adults and those who write primarily for younger readers. I have adopted the same practice here and for similar reasons: it adds richness and variety and it shows that effective and well-told stories work independently of the readers they were first intended for.

Here you will find stories by M. R. James, F. G. Loring, and H. Russell Wakefield, all of whom were writing in the first half of this century, together with contemporary writers for adults including Ramsey Campbell, Angela Carter, and Elizabeth Walter. Alongside these are stories by Adèle Geras, Brian Jacques, Philippa Pearce, and Alison Prince, all of whom write mainly for younger readers.

I hope, of course, that you won't have read any of these stories before. Some will certainly be new to you: those by Marian Abbey, Stephen Elboz, John Gordon, Mick Gowar, Dennis Hamley, and Laurence Staig have been written especially for this collection.

Dennis Pepper
July 1996

Moving House

MARIAN ABBEY

T he house hated her. She knew that. Soon she realized
that she had always known it, even before she moved in.
But what the house wanted wasn't the sort of thing she
was looking out for when she was choosing where to live. Why
should it have been? She had asked about the bus routes, the
shops, the village hall. They all seemed all right. She had
checked the neighbours. They seemed normal, decent, friendly.
She hadn't thought of checking the house.

And it did hate her. It wasn't just her imagination. She had
stood alone in the long narrow hallway and felt the air quiver
about her. The uncomfortable feeling grew, gathered, and
strengthened at the far end of the stairs, and as she walked
towards it the air jostled and murmured like a group of people
she had to push aside.

She fought her way through, elbows out, head down, like the

January Sales, and the air gathered again malevolently behind her and muttered.

Some mornings she would literally keep her head down when she woke to hear the house shift and mutter, It's her again. Trying not to antagonize it, she would wash, dress and eat a quick breakfast standing up in the kitchen—like a guest who knows she's overstayed her welcome but is too hungry not to have some kind of breakfast before she goes. Then she'd get out of the front door quickly, and not return until the next meal. On other days she'd lift her head and look the walls straight in the face, refuse to be intimidated. She would stand at the top of the staircase and call out to that grumbling presence: I'm here, house. I'm here and I'm staying. You can't get rid of me. I don't care what you think.

And once, just once, she had thought that the whole staircase moved and shifted before her eyes, and the banister seemed to resist as she put her weight on it, to steady herself, going down the bucking stairs.

Of course, it was such a pity when the old lady died. That's what everyone in the village had told her, at one time or another. She first heard of it when she came looking for her dream house. Such a lovely old lady. Lived there most of her life, you know. Brought up all her kids there, you know. Three girls and two boys: the house was always full of children. Didn't have much money, not after her old man walked out on them, but there was always space for someone else at the dinner table, the kids were always having friends to stay, there was always laughter.

And now it was just her. No kids; didn't want any. They started out with dirty nappies and screaming red faces, and went on to eat too much and demand money for new clothes. No husband, either; never felt the need for one. But money she wanted, and money she had got. And a big house, a solid house to show she'd arrived and was important and could afford it, that was what she must have. And she was going to stay. For a long time.

The house writhed to get rid of her. Cracks appeared in the walls. She tried to sue the surveyors for not spotting that this was going to happen. But it shouldn't have, they said, puzzled. Must be the dry summer. Tiles twisted themselves off the roof, fell onto her car which was parked below, cutting through the bright red paint to leave shiny metal exposed, like bone. They had a long way to fall. The house was tall, sheer and proud on the west side. She stood and shielded her eyes against the sunlight and looked up. Three storeys of high ceilings. The triangle of roof black and sharp against the sky. She felt a stab of pride. My house. My great, solid house that shows how important and solid I am. I own it. For a moment she forgot to mind about the car. It could be repaired. Heads don't repair so easily, though. Never mind, it missed her: that final tile which dislodged itself, hurtling pointed corner down like a javelin head. She sidestepped it, neatly, and went to phone the insurance company and the garage.

Eventually, when she had lived there for a whole winter, she decided she had had enough. She declared war on the house. It would be hers. All other owners, all previous history, would be forgotten. She phoned the bank manager first, for a loan. She wanted the money now, she explained, a large amount, to spend on the house. She was going to have it done up. Done over.

How do you change someone? You can cut their hair, give them new clothes to wear, teach them to speak in a different voice. She was going to change the house. She brought in painters, plumbers, electricians, carpenters. They banged, hammered, pulled apart and put back together again. They drilled and bashed through walls, pulled up floorboards, painted windows, and put down thick suffocating carpets. They began to alter doorways. The house groaned when they did that. They knocked through one wall to put a new doorway in, and bricked up the door that was already there; and as they did it, she could feel the house resisting her, agonized. The fierce feeling rose up in her and her hands clenched and unclenched until the veins stuck out like wires. She remembered a garden long ago, her little cousin, twisting his wrists until the skin crinkled and burned, her hands hurting him until he promised he would never, ever tell on her again . . .

Now she stood in the front garden and looked at the house. It gazed back at her, warily, with all its window eyes. They were so even, so symmetrical. She had always promised herself that her ideal house would have eight windows. Just the right number. But she knew how to hurt. She narrowed her eyes and smiled. She'd brick up that window on the left. Spoil the house.

That would teach it. No, they weren't eyes, she decided. They were teeth. The front of the house like a mouthful of teeth. Well, she was going to knock one out. Change the whole look of it. See how the house liked that. And then she was going to live in it for ever and ever and there was nothing the house could do about it.

Of course, the villagers had told her how the old lady died. Perhaps it was for the best, after all, they'd said: now that the children were grown up and gone, had left the poor old thing rattling around in a house that was far too big for her. Apart from the look on her face, there was nothing in particular to remark on. Oh, and the bit about where her body was found. Not in her bed. Odd that, because she had difficulty moving around. But for some reason, the night she went, she had got herself out of bed and somehow managed to struggle up the attic stairs, was half-way across the end bedroom as though she was trying to reach something. Whatever it was, it must have been something wonderful, because when they found her, her eyes were fixed on the gable window, and her face was calm and peaceful with such a happy, longing smile. But what she had seen no one could guess. A dream, probably. The window would have been dark. She had died in the middle of the night— her heart gave out, a good way to go, quick, painless release from the arthritis that was twisting her body into agony.

She had never been especially interested in what happened to the old lady. It didn't seem important. Perhaps that was why she never realized, when finally the house turned on her.

It was early spring. The middle of the night. Dark and still so cold that nothing would normally have got her out from under the blankets. But it must have been a dream, probably, that woke her. She lay there in the dark and the atmosphere shook and she called out at the house: You're finished. I've got you. You're mine and I'm going to do whatever I like . . .

Then she heard noises, the most unlikely noises on a cold black night. Children's voices, laughing excitedly, from not very far away. The noise faded and came again, like waves on sand, and just when she thought she had been imagining it there was another lilting sound of children. She got up, out of bed, climbed the stairs. The sound was coming from the top of the house, the empty attic bedroom. It was so dark and yet a line of

light showed under the door, soft light, not very much, not enough for a bulb to have been left on.

She opened the door and stepped into the room. The light grew. The laughter came again. Nothing in the room, but the window glowed with pale green light, the colour of sunlight through leaves, of dew on grass. And out there the children were laughing. She glided across the room, didn't feel the new carpet under her feet. She reached out for the window. She was smiling; she couldn't help it. Spring, and sunlight, and laughter, and children. She opened the window. But it wasn't a window, now, of course; it was a door. A garden door to a different life.

They found her on the concrete, down by the side of the house. Smashed. They couldn't see the expression on her face because her face was gone. They stared up at the house, puzzled. Why ever did she do that? How could she have done it? Climb out of that tiny casement window up there, three floors up there, and jump . . . ?

The Girl in the Mirror

MARGOT ARNOLD

Jennifer Vidler looked around her room with a sigh of boredom.

It was untidy, as usual, but she could not be bothered to tidy it up, even though her mother had been after her to do so. Her friends were always going on about how pretty it was and how lucky she was to have a room like this of her own. Little did *they* know, she thought gloomily. Her eyes wandered over the bleached silver-oak fittings: the built-in wardrobe, the desk, the bookshelves and the stand that held her stereo and television set, and moved on to the gracious lines of her white four-poster bed that seemed almost to float on the thick scarlet wall-to-wall carpet.

She went slowly to the window and gazed down at the busy street below. From this height, cars and people looked like large mechanical toys moving jerkily and without purpose. Oh, what she would give to be away from all this, away from the city! Right away in the country. She slipped easily into her favourite daydream—a big farm in the country with her own horse, and a dog, and cats, and rabbits, and lots of space to roam around in, and—oh, everything! Roaming wild and free all day long with the animals . . . A horn honked outside and the dream shattered.

Again she sighed heavily. Here it was, the beginning of the summer holidays, and all she had to look forward to was a measly fortnight in France with her parents. She was almost sorry that school was finally over—not that she liked school that much, but at least it was something to *do*.

She put another record on the turntable and continued her restless ramble around the room. Coming to the dressing-table with its glass top and white-flounced frill, she stopped before it and, propping her head in her hands, gazed moodily into the mirror. She had made a fuss about it when her mother had put it in the room, but secretly she rather liked it. It had been one of the 'heirlooms' she had inherited from her great-aunt and namesake, Aunt Jennifer, and it did not quite 'go' with the rest of the room, being an antique, shield-shaped, swing-mirror, standing on its own little stand in which were three small velvet-lined drawers where she kept her most cherished possessions.

Every time she looked into it she would think of Aunt Jennifer, who had been incredibly old but who had always interested her with stories about her long-gone youth on a farm in Kent. What especially interested young Jennifer were the stories her great-aunt used to tell about her own grandmother, who had lived on the very same farm way back in the 1830s. She, too, had been a Jennifer, and had had a twin sister called Belinda to whom something terrible had happened.

It had been a very long time before young Jennifer had managed to find out what that terrible thing was, because whenever her great-aunt got to that part some grown-up— usually her own mother—would break in with, 'Now I'm sure you don't want to go into all that, Aunt Jennifer,' and their warning glances were enough to tell her that it was something they did not want her to know about. She had imagined all sorts of horrible things so, when at last she had got Aunt Jennifer all to herself and had heard the story, she had been quite disappointed.

'Oh,' said Aunt Jennifer vaguely, 'about poor Belinda? Yes, well she went quite mad when she was a young girl and had to spend the rest of her life shut up in the farm attic where no one could see her. They didn't know what to do with mad people in those days, you see, and it was a *terrible* disgrace to have one in the family.'

'What made her go mad?' Jennifer asked with interest.

Her great-aunt shrugged. 'My grandmother never knew for sure. She thought maybe it was because their stepmother was too hard on Belinda, who was a very dreamy kind of girl and who wasn't very helpful about the farm. Anyway, one summer's day Belinda started to act very strangely; she pretended she was Jennifer and talked about all kinds of crazy things like talking boxes and wheels that sang songs, and even about men flying about in the sky. It got so bad that they sent the real Jennifer, my grandmother, away for a while, and when she came back poor Belinda was chained up in the attic and she was never allowed to see her again, even though they were twins—and identical twins at that . . .'

Oh yes, Jennifer sorely missed Aunt Jennifer and her stories, but the old lady had died a few months ago and had left her some very nice things.

The door opened and her mother's face appeared around the crack. 'Jennifer, *do* turn down that record-player! We'll have the neighbours complaining again.' The head swivelled and took in the untidy state of the room. 'And for goodness' sake, tidy this mess up, will you? It's the third time I've spoken to you about it.' The voice was pained.

'All right,' Jennifer said sullenly. Her mother sighed and closed the door with an exasperated click.

'Drat the neighbours!' Jennifer resumed her former position and stared dismally into the mirror. 'Oh, how heavenly it must have been to live on that farm, away from everybody!' Her own sad face stared back at her, the long dark hair hanging forward and slightly shadowing its pallor. Then she felt a thrill of amazement, for while the face was the same, the whole room behind was quite different. She glanced quickly over her shoulder to see if her eyes were playing tricks with her, but there was her own room, just the same as it always was. She looked back at the mirror, and the other room was still there— cream walls with great black beams showing in them, and dark, heavy furniture, including a large four-poster bed with a patchwork quilt. And there was a window where no window existed in her room; a window of small, diamond-shaped panes which stood open to show the leaves of a great oak tree dancing in the summer breeze, and there was a door of black oak with a latch instead of a knob on it.

Jennifer took each detail in slowly. How could this be? Here she was looking at her reflection in a strange room! Then she noticed with a shock that while the face was the same, the dress was quite different. The girl in the mirror was wearing a shapeless long dress of some kind of checked cotton, with stupid-looking puffed sleeves out of which her thin arms stuck like sticks. Jennifer glanced down at her own stylish nylon blouse and neat Black Watch kilt, then back at the mirror. 'Who are you?' she whispered through dry lips. 'Why is everything suddenly so different?'

The girl's face—her own face—came a little closer. 'Oh, I'm *so* glad you've finally seen me; that you've said something!' The voice was high and thin and clear like a mountain stream. 'Now we can talk. Now I can find out about all those wonderful things you have that I can see from here. I've been *dying* to know about them.' She gave a delighted laugh that tinkled like a fairy bell. 'What *talks* we'll be able to have now!'

'But . . . *where* are you?' Jennifer stammered.

'Why, on Pear Tree Farm, of course, where I've always been.' The tinkly laugh broke out again. 'And I know who *you* are; there's only one person in the world who looks exactly like me, so you're Jennifer. Don't you know me, silly? I'm Belinda!'

Thrills went up and down Jennifer's spine. 'The farm—the old farm! You're actually on it?'

'Of course.'

Jennifer looked very carefully at her look-alike, thinking of the sad story she had been told. She certainly did not *look* mad, and besides, behind her was the enchanting prospect of the farm. Belinda would be able to tell her all about it. 'Well, I'm not *your* Jennifer,' she said cautiously, 'but I think I know what

has happened. We are both of us caught in a Time Warp—that must be it!' (She was a great fan of *Star Trek*, so knew all about such things.)

'I don't care who you say you are, Jennifer, or what we're caught in, just so long as we can be friends and you can tell me all about those exciting things,' Belinda said eagerly.

'I do know one thing, though,' Jennifer went on. 'We'll have to keep this a *deadly* secret between us. It would never do if anyone else found out.'

'No, indeed!' Belinda made a face and shivered. 'Why, my stepmother is so strict and nasty—well, she'd probably smash this glass if she thought I was having any *fun*.'

So began their strange, looking-glass friendship. Jennifer's parents could hardly believe the change in her; instead of complaining all the time as she usually did in the holidays, she seemed perfectly content to stay in her room; and had almost to be pushed out of the flat to get some fresh air. 'She really is becoming much more grown-up,' her mother said proudly, and as a reward gave her a lovely gold locket with her birth-stone set in the middle of it.

As for Jennifer, she could hardly wait to get back to her room and the mirror, and to hear all the marvellous things about the farm. She would get quite cross with Belinda who, after a while, would always say: 'I've talked enough. Now *you* tell *me* about your wonderful life.' And she could not understand why Belinda should be so impressed by very ordinary things like having a bed all to oneself, and light whenever one needed it, or music at the touch of a switch. 'Imagine! Music whenever you want it—what bliss! I do love it so, and there is none here on the farm, none at all,' Belinda would say sadly.

But most of all it was her television set that really enchanted Belinda, who could not see enough of it and who made Jennifer very angry when she wanted to watch it instead of talking. She got so fed up with Belinda's constant pleas to see it that she would leave it on when she was not in the room, so that Belinda could watch. She was roundly scolded by her mother for wasting electricity, but she still went on doing it.

On her part, although she never tired of hearing about the two riding-horses and the dogs and cats, Jennifer became aware that farm life was not always as nice as she had imagined. Often when she hurried to the mirror Belinda would not be there, and when she did come she would be tired and cross. 'I've been working,' she would say irritably. 'That's all there ever is to do here—work, work, work!' Her hands were always red and raw and quite ugly, but Jennifer was too polite to say so. And she found to her surprise that Belinda was quite ignorant about even the simplest things.

'Don't they teach you *anything* in school,' she said crossly, one day when Belinda seemed even denser than usual.

'School?' echoed Belinda. 'I don't go to school. That's just for *boys*. Though my grandmother did teach me how to make the alphabet and sign my name on a sampler in needlework—*and* I know my figures,' she said proudly. 'I can add! You mean *you* go to school just like a boy, all the time?'

'Well, except for holidays,' Jennifer agreed. 'But it isn't any fun stuck in a stuffy old classroom every day. I *hate* it. You're lucky not to be bothered with it.'

But the more they talked, the more they became envious of each other's life and unhappy with their own; especially Belinda, who would lapse into a gloomy silence and gaze longingly into Jennifer's room. One day when she was doing this, Jennifer cast around in her mind for something new to talk about. She opened up one of the velvet-lined drawers under the mirror and held up the new locket. 'Look what my mother just gave me,' she said.

Belinda brightened up. 'Oh, it's just *beautiful*,' she gasped, and reached for it. For a second a small misty hand appeared, and suddenly there was the locket on the other side of the mirror, with Belinda laughing and twirling it in the air.

'Hey!' said Jennifer. 'You've taken my locket. Give it back!'

Belinda stopped laughing, and a look of wild hope came into her face. 'Jenny,' she whispered, 'it *did* pass through. And if *it* can, maybe *we* can, too! Oh, wouldn't that be fun! I could get into your room and play with all those lovely things, and you could come here and play with the animals—even ride the horses, if you like.'

'Well, I don't know,' Jennifer said dubiously. 'Do you think it would work?'

'Why not? Let's see if I can give the locket back . . .' Again a misty outline appeared, and there was the locket gleaming on the glass top. 'See, Jenny! I believe we could. Let's try it. You put your fingers to mine on the glass and when I say "Go", we'll both take two steps forward.'

The idea had begun to excite Jennifer. 'All right,' she said eagerly, then another thought struck her. 'But wait a moment! What about our clothes? We'd look pretty weird to anyone else. I mean, what would my mother say if she came in and saw you in that cotton sack thing.'

Belinda thought for a minute and chuckled. 'Then we'll take our clothes off, and when we get to the other side we'll dress in one another's. Then, when we're ready to come back, we'll change again.'

Jennifer's heart pounded with excitement. 'Right,' she whispered, and started to undress a bit shamefacedly, her fingers trembling nervously. At last they faced one another, giggling self-consciously at the sight. Belinda, two spots of high colour in her pale cheeks, stretched out her hands. Jenny did the same and took a step forward. For a second she seemed enveloped in an icy mist, where her sight blurred and her senses numbed, then she was standing in that other room, shivering with cold and fear, but excited beyond belief.

Without waiting to dress herself, she ran to the leaded windows, through which drifted the scent of hay and the sounds of summer. She just *had* to see if everything was as Belinda had said it would be.

Sure enough, there was the paddock and the two horses, the grey and the brown, standing head to tail and lazily swishing away the flies. There was the old black and white sheepdog lying in the shade of the barn, and an orange kitten scampering in and out of the wide barn door. So absorbed was she that she paid no attention to a voice from below that was calling on an ever-increasing note of anger: 'Belinda! Belin-dah!'

She ran back to the mirror. 'Oh, Belinda, it's every bit as wonderful as you said . . .' she began, then stopped dead. The shield-shaped glass with its three little drawers stood on a dark oak table, but it did not reflect, as she had expected it to, her own cosy room. Instead, the dark outlines of the farm furniture loomed behind her and—worse—there was no sign of Belinda anywhere.

As she stood there in mounting fear and puzzlement, the

dark shape of a stern-faced woman in black appeared in the doorway, crying, 'Belinda, you lazy good-for-nothing! How many times have I got to call my lungs out before . . .' She stopped short in her scolding as she saw Jennifer crouching naked before the mirror. '*Now* what are you up to, you fiendish girl?' she cried, storming into the room. 'What is the meaning of this wicked nakedness? Wait till I tell your papa of *this*!'

Jennifer cringed back against the traitorous mirror. 'I'm *not* Belinda,' she whimpered, her heart pounding with terror, 'I'm Jennifer, and I want to go home . . .'

The strange disappearance of Jennifer Vidler remains a mystery. No one—least of all the police, who were eventually called in—could explain how a girl could disappear completely from a sixth-floor flat in a large London block; particularly one who apparently was not wearing any of her clothes. At least, this was according to her distracted mother, who had been in the living-room of the flat all the time and swore her daughter never left it, clothed or unclothed.

Nor could they explain why the clothes which she had last been seen wearing were found crumpled in an untidy heap before the dressing-table, nor why there appeared to be on them the print of a small, dusty hand, while beside them was a large mound of dust, which had scattered in a fine film over everything when the door had been opened.

Perhaps the most amazing thing of all was that the mirror on the dressing-table—which, Jennifer's mother had tearfully maintained to the sceptical police, had always been kept as bright and as silver as the day it was made—was all blotched and dark, so that no reflection of any kind could be seen in it.

After a while people gave the whole thing up as an insoluble mystery, but they all said it was just too bad for poor Jennifer, wherever she had got to. How right they were!

Conversion

RAMSEY CAMPBELL

You're in sight of home when you know something's wrong. Moonlight shivers gently on the stream beyond the cottage, and trees stand around you like intricate spikes of the darkness mounting within the forest. The cottage is dark, but it isn't that. You emerge into the glade, trying to sense what's troubling you.

You know you shouldn't have stayed out so late, talking to your friend. Your wife must have been worried, perhaps frightened by the night as well. You've never left her alone at night before. But his talk was so engrossing: you feel that in less than a night you've changed from being wary of him to understanding him completely. And his wine was so good, and his open-throated brightly streaming fire so warming, that you can now remember little except a timeless sense of comfortable companionship, of communion that no longer needed words.

But you shouldn't have left your wife alone in the forest at night, even behind a barred door. The woodcutter's cottage is nearby; at least you could have had his wife to stay with yours. You feel disloyal.

Perhaps that's what has been disturbing you. Always before when you've returned home light has been pouring from the windows, mellowing the surrounding trunks and including them like a wall around your cottage. Now the cottage reminds you of winter nights long ago in your childhood, when you lay listening to a wolf's cry like the slow plummeting of ice into a gorge, and felt the mountains and forests huge around you, raked by the wind. The cottage feels like that: cold and hollow and unwelcoming. For a moment you wonder if you're simply anticipating your wife's blame, but you're sure it's more than that.

In any case you'll have to knock and awaken her. First you go to the window and look in. She's lying in bed, her face open as if to the sky. Moonlight eases darkness from her face, but leaves her throat and the rest of her in shadow. Tears have gathered in her eyes, sparkling. No doubt she has been crying in memory of her sister, a sketch of whom gazes across the bed from beside a glass of water. As you look in you're reminded of your childhood fancy that angels watched over you at night, not at the end of the bed but outside the window; for a second you feel like your wife's angel. But, as you gaze in, discomfort grows in your throat and stomach. You remember how your fancy somehow turned into a terror of glimpsing a white face peering in. You draw back quickly in case you should frighten her.

But you have to knock. You don't understand why you've been delaying. You stride to the door and your fist halts in mid-air, as if impaled by lightning. Suddenly the vague threats and unease you've been feeling seem to rush together and gather on the other side of the door. You know that beyond the door something is waiting for you, ready to pounce.

You feel as if terror has pinned you through your stomach, helpless. You're almost ready to flee into the woods, to free yourself from the skewer of your panic. Sweat pricks you like red-hot ash scattered on your skin. But you can't leave your wife in there with it, whatever nightmare it is rising out of the tales you've heard told of the forest. You force yourself to be still if not calm, and listen for some hint of what it might be.

All you can hear is the slow sleepy breathing of the wind in the trees. Your panic rises, for you can feel it beyond the door, perfectly poised and waiting easily for you to betray yourself. You hurry back to the window, but it's impossible for you to squeeze yourself in far enough to make out anything within the door. This time a stench rises from the room to meet you, trickling into your nostrils. It's so thickly unpleasant that you refuse to think what it might resemble. You edge back, terrified now of awakening your wife, for it can only be her immobility that's protecting her from whatever's in the room.

But you can't coax yourself back to the door. You've allowed your panic to spread out from it, warding you farther from the cottage. Your mind fills with your wife, lying unaware of her plight. Furious with yourself, you compel your body forward against the gale of your panic. You reach the door and struggle to touch it. If you can't do that, you tell yourself, you're a coward, a soft scrabbling thing afraid of the light. Your hand presses against the door as if proving itself against a live coal, and the door swings inwards.

You should have realized that your foe might have entered the cottage through the doorway. You flinch back instinctively, but as the swift fear fades the panic seeps back. You can feel it hanging like a spider just inside the doorway, waiting for you to pass beneath: a huge heavy black spider, ready to plump on your face. You try to shake your panic out of you with the knowledge that it's probably nothing like that, that you're giving in to fancy. But whatever it is, it's oozing a stench that claws its way into your throat and begins to squeeze out your stomach. You fall back, weakened and baffled.

Then you see the rake. It's resting against the corner of the cottage, where you left it after trying to clear a space for a garden. You carry it to the door, thinking. It could be more than a weapon, even though you don't know what you're fighting. If your wife doesn't awaken and draw its attention to her, if your foe isn't intelligent enough to see what you're planning, if your absolute conviction of where it's lurking above the door isn't false—You almost throw away the rake, but you can't bear the sense of your wife's peril any longer. You inch the door open. You're sure you have only one chance.

You reach stealthily into the space above the door with the

teeth of the rake, then you grind them into your prey and drag it out into the open. It's a dark tangled mass, but you hurl it away into the forest without looking closer, for some of it has fallen into the doorway and lies dimly there, its stench welling up. You pin it with the teeth and fling it into the trees.

Then you realize there's more, hanging and skulking around the side of the door-frame. You grab it with the rake and hurl it against a trunk. Then you let your breath roar out. You're weak and dizzy, but you stagger through the doorway. There are smears of the thing around the frame and you sway back, retching. You close your mouth and nostrils and you're past, safe.

You lean on the rake and gaze down at your wife. There's a faint stench clinging to the rake, and you push it away from you, against the wall. She's still asleep, no doubt because you were mourning her sister all last night. Your memory's blurring; you must be exhausted too, because you can remember hardly anything before the battle you've just fought. You're limply grateful that no harm has befallen her. If she'd come with you to visit your friend none of this would have happened. You hope you can recapture the sense of communion you had with him, to pass on to your wife. Through your blurring consciousness you feel an enormous yearning for her.

Then you jerk alert, for there's still something in the room. You glance about wildly and see beneath the window more of what you destroyed, lying like a tattered snake. You manage to scoop it up in one piece this time, and you throw the rake out with it. Then you turn back to your wife. You've disturbed her; she has moved in her sleep. And fear advances on you from the bed like a spreading stain pumped out by a heart, because now you can see what's nestling at her throat.

You don't know what it is; your terror blurs it and crowds out your memories until it looks like nothing you've ever seen. It rests in the hollow of her throat like a dormant bat, and indeed it seems to have stubby protruding wings. Its shape expands within your head until it is a slow explosion of pure hostility, growing and erasing you. You turn away, blinded.

It's far worse than what you threw into the forest. Even then, if you hadn't been fighting for your wife you would have been

paralysed by superstition. Now you can hardly turn your head back to look. The stain of the thing is crawling over your wife, blotting out her face and all your sense of her. But you open your eyes an agonized slit and see it couched in her throat as if it lives there. Your rage floods up, and you start forward.

But even with your eyes closed you can't gain on it, because a great cold inhuman power closes about you, crushing you like a moth in a fist. You mustn't cry out, because if your wife awakens it may turn on her, and you hear her awake.

Your seared eyes make out her face, dimmed by the force of the thing at her neck. Perhaps her gathered tears are dislodged, or perhaps these are new, wrung out by the terror in her eyes. Your head is a shell full of fire, your eyes feel as though turning to ash, but you battle forward. Then you realize she's shrinking back. She isn't terrified of the thing at her throat at all, she's terrified of you. She's completely in its power.

You're still straining against the force, wondering whether it must divert some of its power from you in order to control her, when she grabs the glass from beside the bed. For a moment you can't imagine what she wants with a glass of water. But it isn't water. It's vitriol, and she throws it in your face.

Your face bursts into pain. Howling, you rush to the mirror.

You're still searching for yourself in the mirror when the woodcutter appears in the doorway, grim-faced. At once, like an eye in the whirlwind of your confusion and pain, you remember that you asked his wife to stay with yours, yesterday afternoon when he wasn't home to dissuade you from what you had to do. And you know why you can't see yourself, only the room and the doorway through which you threw the garlic, your sobbing wife clutching the cross at her throat, the glass empty now of the holy water you brought home before setting out to avenge her sister's death at Castle Dracula.

The Werewolf

ANGELA CARTER

It is a northern country; they have cold weather, they have cold hearts.

Cold; tempest; wild beasts in the forest. It is a hard life. Their houses are built of logs, dark and smoky within. There will be a crude icon of the virgin behind a guttering candle, the leg of a pig hung up to cure, a string of drying mushrooms. A bed, a stool, a table. Harsh, brief, poor lives.

To these upland woodsmen, the Devil is as real as you or I. More so; they have not seen us nor even know that we exist, but the Devil they glimpse often in the graveyards, those bleak and touching townships of the dead where the graves are marked with portraits of the deceased in the naïf style and there are no flowers to put in front of them, no flowers grow there, so they put out small, votive offerings, little loaves, sometimes a cake that the bears come lumbering from the margins of the forest to snatch away. At midnight, especially on *Walpurgisnacht*, the Devil holds picnics in the graveyards and invites the witches; then they dig up fresh corpses, and eat them. Anyone will tell you that.

Wreaths of garlic on the doors keep out the vampires. A blue-eyed child born feet first on the night of St John's Eve will have second sight. When they discover a witch—some old woman whose cheeses ripen when her neighbours' do not, another old woman whose black cat, oh, sinister! *follows her about all the time*, they strip the crone, search for her marks, for the supernumerary nipple her familiar sucks. They soon find it. Then they stone her to death.

Winter and cold weather.

Go and visit grandmother, who has been sick. Take her the oatcakes I've baked for her on the hearthstone and a little pot of butter.

The good child does as her mother bids—five miles' trudge through the forest; do not leave the path because of the bears, the wild boar, the starving wolves. Here, take your father's hunting knife; you know how to use it.

The child had a scabby coat of sheepskin to keep out the cold, she knew the forest too well to fear it but she must always be on her guard. When she heard that freezing howl of a wolf, she dropped her gifts, seized her knife and turned on the beast.

It was a huge one, with red eyes and running, grizzled chops; any but a mountaineer's child would have died of fright at the sight of it. It went for her throat, as wolves do, but she made a great swipe at it with her father's knife and slashed off its right forepaw.

The wolf let out a gulp, almost a sob, when it saw what had happened to it; wolves are less brave than they seem. It went lolloping off disconsolately between the trees as well as it could on three legs, leaving a trail of blood behind it. The child wiped the blade of her knife clean on her apron, wrapped up the wolf's paw in the cloth in which her mother had packed the oatcakes and went on towards her grandmother's house. Soon it came on to snow so thickly that the path and any footsteps, track or spoor that might have been upon it were obscured.

She found her grandmother was so sick she had taken to her

bed and fallen into a fretful sleep, moaning and shaking so that the child guessed she had a fever. She felt the forehead, it burned. She shook out the cloth from her basket, to use it to make the old woman a cold compress, and the wolf's paw fell to the floor.

But it was no longer a wolf's paw. It was a hand, chopped off at the wrist, a hand toughened with work and freckled with old age. There was a wedding ring on the third finger and a wart on the index finger. By the wart, she knew it for her grandmother's hand.

She pulled back the sheet but the old woman woke up, at that, and began to struggle, squawking and shrieking like a thing possessed. But the child was strong, and armed with her father's hunting knife; she managed to hold her grandmother down long enough to see the cause of her fever. There was a bloody stump where her right hand should have been, festering already.

The child crossed herself and cried out so loud the neighbours heard her and came rushing in. They knew the wart on the hand at once for a witch's nipple; they drove the old woman, in her shift as she was, out into the snow with sticks, beating her old carcass as far as the edge of the forest, and pelted her with stones until she fell down dead.

Now the child lived in her grandmother's house; she prospered.

Goodman's Tenants

MICHAEL CHISLETT

It was the first time that Dalton had visited Suffolk; the first time with his metal detector, at any rate. He walked along the shoreline, the wind from the sea blowing through his thinning, sandy hair. The wrack from yesterday's storm littered the beach, while the grey waves of the receding tide fell with a steady, sullen hiss on the sand.

He had long meant to try the Suffolk coast—others who shared his enthusiasm had spoken of the decent finds one might make along that ancient, haunted shore, especially in the wake of storms. The devastating tempest that had ravaged the eastern counties over the last few days had persuaded him, and he had decided on impulse to drive up from London and try his luck.

So far, two hours of walking along the shore had netted him several rusty nails, two tenpence pieces and a half-crown dated 1957. Plenty of wood lay cast about, for the storm had stirred and broken-up many old wrecks, but there was nothing that could be easily identified. It was just old, rotting driftwood, black and dripping with seaweed, which lay dark and sinister on the light sand, like the hair of a drowned witch.

The wind blew, sharp and piercing. Dalton had fashioned earplugs from cotton wool, knowing that the wind blowing into his ears would make him deaf for days. The earplugs also muffled the sound of the waves and the cries of the sea birds, which tore at the flesh of dead and stranded fish strewn along the beach. To his left were the remains of low cliffs, crumbled and eroded, spilling down to the beach. Rocks and stones, turned an underwater green by the washing tide, lay strewn about like the remains of some long lost city that had been claimed in anger by the sea gods. On the cliff top long grass waved wildly in the wind. The cliff became nothing more than low dunes after less than half a mile, suggesting to Dalton grave-mounds left by some long-vanished race. The waterline reached right up to them, and with every storm he knew that a little more land would be claimed by the sea.

How long, he wondered, before the whole of this flat land would be inundated? Once there had been cities along the shore: prosperous Saxon and Roman towns which were now but a folk memory, legendary places which the unappeasable waters had claimed. It was possible that the dunes covered the remains of a village, for there seemed to be a definite shape to some of the mounds. It might prove profitable to abandon the beach and try the cliff, or the rocks at its base.

Just behind the cliff top Dalton saw what he at first took to be someone waving to him. He screwed up his eyes to look; then gave a laugh as he realized it was only a scarecrow, leaning precariously over the top of the cliff. The rags of its clothing flapped in the wind, as if it was about to fly down from its perch.

The metal detector gave a high-pitched beep, and Dalton turned his attention to it, weaving a circle over the source of the sound. Finding the exact spot, he took out a small spade from his rucksack and began to dig carefully around it. After some minutes he disgustedly pulled out a rusty tin can, which he threw to join the other litter on the beach.

He straightened up and looked back at the cliffs and dunes.

The scarecrow seemed to have gone—probably blown away in the wind, he thought. He'd try his luck up there, he decided; it certainly couldn't be any worse than on the beach. And in the dunes he would be out of the wind somewhat. The leaden sky promised rain, and he didn't want to be far from his car when it started. Yes: he would try the dunes, then make his way back along the cliff. Perhaps an interesting find could be made along there.

The sand was much softer among the dunes, and made for heavy going as it sucked against his wellingtons and shifted away beneath his feet. Still the detector found nothing. The ground began to rise away from the dunes and became firmer, and Dalton, spotting a rough track, began to follow it up.

He kept well to the inland side of the path, for it ran a little too close to the crumbling edge for his liking, and he had an aversion to sheer drops, however short. A violent gust of wind caused him to stagger slightly, giving him even more incentive to avoid the edge, and he moved a bit closer to the fenced fields that bordered the landward side of the path. He started up his detector once more, and slowly and methodically covered the ground as he walked.

The track ended abruptly where the cliff had fallen away. Dalton looked cautiously down and saw that part of it must have collapsed during the night, for fresh rock and soil lay spread over the sand of the beach below. The only possible way to continue would be to climb over the fence into the adjacent field, which he did. It was slow going over the wet, ploughed earth, and his boots were soon ankle-deep in churned-up mud. So intent was he on his progress that he did not notice a man standing on the pathway until he reached a point where he could climb over the fence and regain the track. The man was staring gloomily at the spot where the track had fallen.

'It'll take my field next,' he said, sweeping his arm in a wide gesture to indicate the sea. He stared out over the water, and Dalton felt that it was up to him to say something.

'Sorry, but I had to walk across your field.' He indicated the washed-out part of the track. 'There was no other way around. I was doing a bit of detecting along the beach, and then along the path.' He stopped, unsure of how much further to go. He knew that farmers didn't always take kindly to people with metal detectors poking about their land without permission.

The man turned to look at him. 'Find anything?'

'Only this.' Dalton fished about in his pocket and produced the half-crown.

'Not been a very good day for you, then. There used to be better pickings in the old days.'

'Yes, I suppose there are a lot of people out with metal detectors now. Too much competition.'

The farmer laughed drily. 'No, I didn't mean metal detectors. There used to be folks hereabouts would go out after a storm and see what ships had been driven ashore. They'd loot the wrecks, and if there were any survivors: well, the ones the sea didn't get would be dispatched pretty sharpish, and buried quickly. Out of sight, out of mind. Colourful local history, but not something you find in the tourist books.' He paused, as if he had said too much, and changed the subject. 'Will you be continuing along the cliffs?'

Dalton nodded.

'The track is fine from here,' the farmer said, 'but keep away from the edge. Do you see that enclosed field a bit further along?'

Dalton looked in the direction the man indicated, and thought he saw a movement, like a sheet tossed in the wind. Something grey blew across the field: much too large to be a bird, he thought, and surely not a sheep. It had seemed to be upright, and moving with a sinister dancing step over the low hummocks of grass. He rubbed his eyes, which were watering badly in the wind. It could have been anything, or nothing.

'Whatever you do, don't try to cross that field,' the farmer was advising. 'It's dangerous.'

Dalton looked again, and realized that what he had seen tumbling about in the wind was a scarecrow. It moved agitatedly in the wind, then collapsed to the ground. Beyond the field, and separated from it by another fence, was another, larger field, covered with hummocks of what looked like stone.

'Did there used to be a building there?' he asked. The farmer nodded.

'Used to be a church there, long before I was born. It collapsed in a storm, and what wasn't taken away for use by the locals was left behind where it fell. Not in that first field, though. *That* was never part of the churchyard.' He looked at Dalton sharply. 'There's notices up on the fence, warning people to keep out, so there's no excuse for going in.'

The farmer's words caused Dalton to feel a perverse interest in the field. 'Is it used for anything, that first field?' he asked.

'It's Goodman's field,' the man replied, as if that were answer enough. Then he added vehemently, 'I wish the sea would take the bloody place.'

He turned abruptly away from Dalton and climbed over the fence into his own field. At first Dalton thought he would walk away without another word; then he turned, and said once more, 'Remember: stick to the path, and you'll be all right. Don't go in the field.' Then he turned and trudged away.

Dalton called out a thank you, and began to make his way along the path. The metal detector, however, stayed obstinately silent, and he turned his attention to his surroundings. Out to sea the waves were growing heavier, as if the tide was about to turn. The fields to his left were full of nothing but mud and long grass, as if abandoned and left uncultivated.

Except, that was, for the first of the two fields the farmer had pointed out to him. He could see the scarecrow plainly now. Perhaps the wind was playing with it, knocking it down and plucking it up at random. Indeed, he could see two more at the far end of the enclosed ground. Strange that there were so many bird scarers in a place that was so obviously neglected.

The thought of visiting the field, after the farmer's warnings to keep away, had become strangely enticing. It would be good to sit out of the biting wind for a time, and there looked to be some shelter against the fence where he could sit and have a sandwich and some coffee. The only alternative was to go back to his car, but if he did that he might as well go home. He looked at the grey sea, rolling heavily with the storm which had not yet spent its fury.

'Glad I'm not a sailor on a day like this,' he thought. 'Or have a house on the edge of the cliff.'

The field had looked close enough when he had been talking to the farmer, but it seemed to take him a peculiarly long time to get there. He finally reached its edge, however, and looked over the fence at the hummocks of grass swaying in the wind. Stones showed white through the earth, and scrubby, mean bushes barely found sustenance in the rocky ground. Other stones—black and lichen-encrusted, some large but most of them small and broken—were casually strewn about, reminding him of the bomb sites of his London childhood.

In the field beyond he could clearly make out the hummocks of stone where the remains of the old church lay, buried and forgotten. The ground had been badly broken up, forming small gullies and holes like hollows in the earth. Who knew what treasures could be concealed here? Why, the Middleham jewel had been discovered in just such a place as this. Dalton had dreamed of that big find which had so far eluded him. Now he was filled with the certainty that in these fields he would find something. He had heard before of other treasure-seekers having sudden flashes of intuition. Getting into the fields had become an obsession.

There was, as the farmer had said, a notice on the fence, but the elements had obliterated the writing on it, and the message was indecipherable. All that was recognizable was something at the bottom of the sheet, which looked like a crude representation of a skull and crossbones. This, however, appeared to have been drawn independently of the printed message, whatever it might have said.

There was no sign of a gate, so Dalton lifted his gear over the fence and dropped it as gently as he could on the other side. The incongruous figure of the scarecrow suddenly blew upwards again, rags flapping as it performed some stationary, admonitory dance. The others on the far side of the field shook themselves with equal violence as if in reply.

Dalton climbed over the fence with some difficulty. Now that he was standing inside the field he could see that it was distinctly lower than on the cliff side of the fence. It had a peculiar effect on perspective: the field appeared to be longer and much broader than it had when viewed from the other side.

He felt a mounting sense of excitement. This was just the place for treasure hunting: the spot he had always dreamt of discovering. The thought that it might have been picked over by scores of others with the same idea did not occur to him. Goodman's field, the farmer had called it. Would the eponymous Goodman mind him intruding on his land? Too

bad if he did. Dalton could always plead ignorance of the field's ownership. But there seemed little chance of being discovered: there was no one in sight save the scarecrows, which leaned against the fence as if bracing their ragged, stick-like bodies against the wind.

Dalton found a place beneath the fence which seemed to be dry and out of the wind. Taking a thermos from his rucksack, he poured out a steaming cup of coffee. That and a sandwich, he thought; then he would start.

Anticipation of what he might find gave Dalton a keen appetite. The day had been dismal and unrewarding so far, but he felt sure that his luck was about to change. Today he would make that big find. Over the years he had turned up some decent stuff and made a bit of money from the dealers in the Portobello Road and Caledonian markets, but nothing really exceptional. He wondered again about whether or not the field's owner would object. Perhaps it still belonged to the church; but no, the farmer had said it wasn't church land.

It was not much of a worry: he could smooth-talk any farmer. The land was so rough and broken that it surely couldn't be used for anything, which meant that the chance of being disturbed by an irate owner was remote. The place had never been under cultivation: that was obvious, even to a Cockney like himself. Long, wind-swept grass and weed covered the rock-strewn ground. Not really the best place to use a metal detector; but it was obvious that the earth had lain undisturbed for ages.

'And that is the way we like it.'

Dalton looked around in surprise. The wind was making him hear things. He took the cotton wool out of his ears and rubbed them vigorously, as if trying to dislodge the words that had been murmured there. The sudden change in the level of sound made him dizzy, and he leaned back against the fence to steady himself. The shrieking of the wind almost decided him to pack up and go. But he had to find something: anything.

There had to be some reason why the field was fenced off so securely. Maybe it was dangerous in some way; perhaps there were deep holes hidden in the ground. The farmer had warned him, and there was that notice on the fence. Of course, there was always an element of risk involved when exploring a new place—but the thought of falling into a hole and lying there for days with a broken leg was not pleasant.

'Ah well: no pain, no gain,' he said aloud, climbing to his feet and turning on the metal detector. He began to sweep it in a circle over the ground.

'Gain by our pain.'

The words seemed to be carried on the wind, and Dalton stopped to look suspiciously around him. He was quite alone in the field; except, of course, for the scarecrows. How many had there been before—two, or three? Now there seemed to be several more leaning against the fence, long lank hair blowing over their round, grey, blank faces. He was about to take a closer look at them—one, at least, seemed to be moving, sliding forward as if blown by the wind—when a sudden beeping from the machine made him look down.

There was something there. Pinpointing the position, he took out his spade and began to dig. Who knew what might be there? Gold, jewellery, items of wonderful, intricate workmanship hidden for centuries. Or nails. He cursed.

There were quite a few of them, though, very near the surface: rusty and fragile, some still set in rotting, spongy wood. Perhaps it was a chest of some kind? No, there was nothing else.

With a sharp cry he drew his hand back. One of the nails, like a vindictive claw covered in rust and dirt, had cut into his flesh. Blood from the wound welled across the palm of his left hand, and he walked quickly towards the spot where he had left his rucksack, blood dripping from his hand and soaking into the earth. Luckily, he came prepared for this sort of emergency, with bandages and T.C.P., but now he would have the bother of going to the hospital for a tetanus injection. Those damned nails could have been there for centuries. Who knew what diseases they might carry, or what he might pick up from the scratch. He pulled a handkerchief from his pocket and wrapped it around his hand.

Finding the bag was not proving to be as easy as he had thought. The geography of the field was confusing him. Surely he hadn't strayed more than a few yards from where he had left the rucksack, but it was nowhere in sight. It should have been beside the fence, where he had sat; but just where that had been was now impossible to tell.

His hand was aching abominably from the cut, and the handkerchief he had wrapped around it had become scarlet and sodden. He sat down, suddenly feeling horribly weak, and tried desperately to orientate himself. If he walked directly towards the sea, he would reach the fence; then it would be a simple matter of making a circuit until he found his rucksack. He rested for another moment, then stood upright and took a deep breath, trying to overcome his dizziness. His glance fell on a large piece of stone which lay on the ground near where he had sat, and he tried to think of what it looked like. A cross; that was it. The top of a cross, crudely carved but unmistakable. It took a few moments for realization to sink into his pain-fogged mind.

'I'm in a bloody graveyard!'

That explained all the nails, so close to the surface. He shuddered at the thought of what they must have held down. But hadn't the farmer said that this land had never been part of the churchyard? What sort of people were buried in unconsecrated land? People who were buried hastily and surreptitiously; people about whose death there were some doubts.

'Out of sight, out of mind.'

The farmer's words came back to him, and Dalton felt a sense of panic welling up inside him. He had to get out of this place. His rational mind told him that it could only be a few dozen yards to the fence, but all perspective seemed to be altered. The sea appeared to have drawn back to the horizon, as though it shrank with horror from the land, while the wild shriek of the wind and the sinister cries of the seabirds were loud one moment and ominously silent the next.

Dalton closed his eyes for a moment and tried to pull himself together. The wound in his hand must be causing the hallucinations. Who would have thought so much blood could flow from such a small cut? Obviously the nail must have been infected with something. With a groan he tried to move, and took an unsteady step in what he hoped was the general direction of the sea. Instinct told him that if he could find some exit from the field he would be all right.

Staggering along, holding his bloody, dripping hand in the other, Dalton saw his rucksack at last. Surely it was not in the place he had left it, though: for there had been no scarecrow standing near the spot where he had sat down.

The thing was definitely standing there now, its ragged and flapping arms outspread as if to prevent Dalton from going further. The mouth was an unpleasant, sardonic grin, but fortunately most of what there was of the face was hidden by tangled, matted hair, like an upturned mop. The black hollow where the nose should have been seemed to be sniffing, as if it caught the scent of some victim. It moved its head, and the hair fell back from the face, showing eye sockets that burned with a feral gleam of implacable hatred.

Dalton turned, to see the others advancing towards him. He was about to meet the field's tenants, who obviously had no good intentions towards trespassers on their domain.

They walked with the sinister, stiff-legged gait of those whose muscles and sinews had long turned rigid and leathery. Dalton wondered how he had mistaken them for anything but what they were. Goodman's field, the farmer had called the place. No doubt the locals knew better than to give the place a better, truer name.

Wishing that he could close his eyes and shut them out as they came closer, Dalton's last rational thought was how sickening their smell was. His scream was lost in the howl of the wind as strong, bony fingers began to scratch and tear.

Mother

STEPHEN ELBOZ

Abully cannot exist without a victim. His bully-bait. And Robert Spry was pure bully-bait. Small, thin, his glasses held together with sticky-tape after the last time Ashley Polebrook had broken them. It didn't help Robert's cause that he was good at school while his bully most definitely was not. It simply added fuel to the fire—the long slow burn until hometime, when his bully showed him what really mattered in this world was the hardness of the punch or a well aimed kick.

Dim witted, Robert's bully never varied his routine. He always waited in that scrub of spindly trees he knew Robert had to cross, blocking the pathway, pretending at first not to notice Robert, as if Robert was too insignificant.

There he stood now, fists in pockets. Seeing him, even at a distance, brought the tightness to Robert's chest. Yet he knew better than to try to run. He slowed up, then stopped.

'I . . . I've no money,' he half whispered after a long silence, his eyes lowered and speaking to the ground. He had learned that he couldn't buy off his bully, that the money was taken in an atmosphere of utter contempt which often made his torment worse.

'Who says I *wants* your stinking money?'

Robert realized he had said the wrong thing. The bully was advancing. Robert felt prickly heat rise from his spine and a second later a blow to his shoulder sent him stumbling backwards into the mud. His bag fell open and books dropped out. The bully took pleasure in stamping them further into the mud. Robert watched him passively, his glasses slightly askew.

The bully snatched up an exercise book fluttering half out of the bag as if trying to fly away in panic.

With a sneer he cast his eyes over Robert's neatly written script on its front cover and sarcastically read, 'The members of the big cat family by Robert G. Spry.' Roughly he thumbed its pages, hardly glancing at what was written there, or at Robert's detailed drawings. Robert winced. Please, he thought, don't damage it. Any of the other books—or even a blow or a kick—but please don't damage that *one* book.

Several months ago there had been a small class project about big cats, which for Robert had quickly grown from an interest into a consuming passion. Even then, of all the cat family, panthers had been his favourites: they were simply so beautiful. They could kill a man in their stride.

Recognizing Robert's passion, Mr Leeson had given him the exercise book for the specific purpose of recording all his information. Now, most dinner times, Robert was to be found in the school library searching out even the tiniest detail about cats; and, of course, the library was one place where his bully never ventured.

Like all expert bullies, Ashley Polebrook sensed the worth to his victim of the prize he gripped in his hands. Smiling coldly he held it before Robert's face, slowly tearing it into four neat pieces and scattering them on the ground. As if they offended his tormentor's sight, Robert immediately leapt up to clear everything away.

The bully spat into the mud. 'Why don't you just clear off home to your mummy, Spry?'

Robert paused, looking at him, for a second on the verge of speaking. But what was there to say? That at home he had tried to explain about his bully to his mother and all that she had said was, 'You must be doing something to draw attention to yourself'? It was then Robert realized his mother saw him as a victim too and thereafter felt only coldness towards her.

He turned and ran home, if only for the security of solid walls and doors he could lock. In the kitchen his mother was chopping carrots with the same indifference she did everything. She gave him a glance.

'You're all mud,' she said flatly.

'Football.'

'Again?'

'Tripped.'

'Plain clumsy.'

She picked up the last piece of carrot and crunched it. Robert watched her, wishing she would ask more, but knowing she wouldn't.

Later, after a silent gloomy meal and an attempt to clean up the mud and repair the ripped book that was way beyond repairing, Robert slipped away to his room. Only here did he feel entirely safe, his mother rarely venturing past its door. As always the room was fastidiously tidy, Robert taking pleasure in order—from the books on the shelf to the shoes by the bed. He kept it so, hoping that his mother might come by and notice . . .

He switched on his computer, the monitor lighting an otherwise dark room. It was time to transfer today's findings on to disk. Carefully he turned the pieces of mud-stained pages, wondering why the book meant so much to him when most of its details were already logged in his computer and he knew them off by heart in any case. Perhaps it was because he would have nothing to show Mr Leeson—the only one who ever took the slightest interest in him. Tomorrow Robert would have to invent some excuse to explain why he no longer had the book, making sure he didn't implicate his bully in the matter. A good victim never does that.

Angrily Robert found himself striking the keyboard. The screen glowed information. Today at school he had discovered about panther cubs and how they are reared.

He typed: *Panthers can have two maybe three cubs. Panthers make ferociously protective mothers, often defending their cubs to the death* . . .

He stopped abruptly with a sense of pain, his glasses shining with reflected light.

'Panthers will defend *their* own young. They'd fight come what may to protect them. A panther mother wouldn't just stand by and watch *her* cubs being harmed.'

The bitterness of his words spoken aloud to the monitor surprised him. But only for a moment. The computer's screen had suddenly turned into a hissing snow storm of interference. Its brightness made him draw back and its hiss was like that of some living creature. Then, just as abruptly, it failed altogether.

Sitting blind before the unresponsive keyboard, Robert felt the darkness brush against him. And more. Something wet and coarse like a tongue was slowly drawing itself across the back of his neck. Frozen with terror, he could hear his blood throbbing and was quite unable to move. Many minutes passed before he was convinced that nothing was there, or ever had been. When finally he dared to move and switched on the light, his room mocked him with its orderliness. For a brief moment Robert felt disappointed.

He was awoken the following morning by his mother's scream. As his mother was not one to raise a noise about anything, this added to the urgency of Robert's haste as he dashed downstairs into the kitchen. His mother stood at the half-opened back door. Under her raised arm Robert could see the step and the vividness of blood. Less obvious was the pathetic heap nearby. Robert tilted his head and saw it was a freshly slaughtered lamb.

Instinctively he thought of his bully and that it must have been left there by him. But no: Ashley Polebrook was always more direct in his cruelty. Robert took another step forward. The dead lamb, he observed, was set down neatly, almost like an offering. Then, recalling the touch in the darkness like a slow deliberate lick, Robert smiled.

The police hadn't yet arrived about the matter of the dead lamb when Robert set off for school. He didn't mind leaving, for he sensed he carried the drama with him; and, as he ran, he felt light headed, revelling in a sense of power. Occasionally he caught a shadowy movement in the bushes alongside the path, keeping in complete step with him.

And look. Before him—on the path. Waiting. Ashley Polebrook. His loyal bully.

Mistaking his speed for an attempt to escape, Ashley grabbed Robert's collar. Robert felt the stitches give.

'You better let me be, Polebrook,' he said, breathless still from running.

His unexpected insolence took a while to register in the bully's slow brain and become a contemptuous expression on his face. He yanked Robert closer to him.

'Why? What you goin' to do about it, Spry? Tell your mummy on me?'

Robert blinked. 'Yes,' he said softly.

And in the bushes arose the crackle of twigs and a long deep-throated growl.

Captain Ashe's Daughter

ADÈLE GERAS

Every Thursday afternoon at 2.30, Bridget Carney presented herself at Holmecroft Old People's Home and made her way across the beige carpet in the Sun Lounge to where Sybil Meadows always sat. Sybil was one of Holmecroft's oldest residents and very proud of her status.

'I'm as old as the century,' she told Bridget on her very first visit. 'Ninety-four next birthday and I've never been further than Blackpool all my life. And what's more . . .' (she raised her voice so that no one should miss what she was about to say) 'I might be weak, but I've still got all my marbles, unlike some old fossils I could mention!'

That was true. 'Sybil's quite a character,' Matron had said. 'Got the gift of the gab, that one, and no mistake. Start her off on a story and there's no stopping her.'

Bridget thought Sybil was a little cheeky, speaking as she did about all the other old folks. At first, the sight of so many elderly people together in one room, nodding, trembling, staring at you curiously, was a little unnerving, but Bridget had grown used to coming to Holmecroft and most of the time she enjoyed her afternoons with Sybil.

Bridget's visits were part of her Sixth Form College's 'Care in the Community' Scheme. She had undertaken to read to Sybil for a couple of hours every Thursday afternoon but when she'd volunteered, she'd imagined novels, stories, anything from Charles Dickens to Mills and Boon. She had certainly never thought that the *South Manchester Reporter* was going to be what Sybil wished to hear. There wasn't anything wrong with the *South Manchester Reporter*, but when you'd read every single letter (about wheelie bins, muggers, Pets' Corner in Fog Lane Park, etc., etc.) and every single local news item, including most of the advertising copy and what was showing at Cinecity this week, you did begin to long for narrative of some kind. Next week, Bridget vowed to herself as she turned over to page four, I'll suggest a book. Maybe I'll bring one. I'll ask Gran what she likes.

'Cat got your tongue, Bridget?' Sybil asked. 'Why aren't you reading?'

'Just turning over, Miss Meadows,' said Bridget. 'Here we go: "Didsbury mansion bought by Computer Firm." That's the headline. "Willow Grange, once the home of cotton merchant Isaac Winterthorne, has been standing empty for some time now . . ."'

'Stop!' said Sybil. 'Did you say Willow Grange?'

'Yes.'

'Oh my,' said Sybil, almost whispering. 'Willow Grange. I thought I'd left that far, far behind me, and now here it is again.'

'Do you know the house?' Bridget asked.

'Know it? Oh, yes. I was there almost from the beginning. The house had just been built. I went into service at Willow Grange when I was fourteen years old. The war had just started. I mean the First War, of course. The Great War. It was supposed to be over by Christmas, you know, but it wasn't. I was to be parlourmaid, only Miss Isabel, who was Isaac Winterthorne's daughter, took a fancy to me, and wanted to train me as her

lady's maid. I'd never seen a house like Willow Grange before
. . . not from the inside. There were floors with parquet tiles on
them like satin (and they need a lot of polishing, I can tell you
that!) and chandeliers that hung down from the ceiling, and all
those little tinkly crystal bits needed dusting, and once a year
Johnson, the butler, used to take them down with a special
gadget that had a hook on the end of it. We spent hours washing
the dratted things. Then there were the Turkey rugs to be
shaken out (no Hoovers, my dear, not in 1914) and meals
seemed to take all day, what with cooking them, serving them,
and washing up afterwards. Still, I was happy at Willow
Grange. I had a black dress and a white pinafore, and the
Winterthornes were good to me, when they noticed I was there.
Best of all, though, there was Miss Isabel. We took to one
another straight away. She was only a few years older than me
. . . seventeen when I arrived at the house, and she'd chat to me
as I brushed her hair or tidied her room, just as if I were her
sister. We used to take walks around the garden after lunch. I'd
never seen a garden like that, not before I went there, and not
often since. I was born in a street where the red-brick houses
were built back-to-back, and if you saw a tree once a year, you
counted yourself lucky. The garden at Willow Grange was a
paradise: banks of rhododendron so thick that you couldn't see
the back of the house from the street, and lawns like the baize
on the master's billiard table in the Games Room, and the
flowerbeds full of rose-bushes with never a leaf out of place,
and borders full of such colours, and butterflies on all the
shrubs in summer, and of course, the artificial lake.'

'They mention a lake,' said Bridget. 'In the article. Listen:
"The original owner had an ornamental lake made in the
grounds, and the willow trees which were planted around it
gave the house its name."'

'That's true enough,' said Sybil, 'but lake's a bit too big a
word, to my mind. It was more of a pond really. In the Japanese
style. It was full of waterlilies, and there was a little wooden
bridge over the water that Miss Isabel and I used to like to stand
on. On really sunny days you could see the goldfish, swimming
about among the tangled roots of the waterlilies.'

'Where is this Willow Grange?' Bridget asked. 'I've never
seen it.'

'Oh, well, it was always well-hidden. There's lots of houses in Didsbury not everybody knows about. Willow Grange is behind Barlow Moor Road, down by the Mersey. You'd never find it if you weren't looking.'

'Why hasn't it been lived in for so long?' Bridget wanted to know. 'If it's so posh and everything?'

Sybil stared into space for such a long time that Bridget was on the point of calling for Matron. Then she said quietly, 'It wouldn't surprise me a bit if that place was haunted.'

'You're not serious!' Bridget laughed. 'You don't mean ghosts, do you? Your actual white floaty kind?'

'There's ghosts and ghosts,' Sybil said. 'All I know is, after what happened Mr and Mrs Winterthorne didn't fancy living there any more and who could blame them?'

'What *did* happen? Do tell me,' said Bridget.

'What about the rest of my newspaper, though?' Sybil asked. 'When'll I hear that?'

'This is more exciting than anything in the paper, honestly.'

'Exciting? Perhaps. The Winterthornes left Willow Grange and after that it became some kind of school, and then an old people's home, but nothing ever lasted very long there, and lately, well . . . I hadn't heard anything about it for years and years and I'd forgotten all about it, you might say, only forgotten is the wrong word. I remember everything perfectly, only I've pushed it to the back of my mind, so as not to have to think about it too much. I do dream about it sometimes, though.'

Bridget suppressed a sigh. At this rate, dragging the story out of Sybil was going to take hours and hours.

'Tell me all about it,' she said encouragingly. 'I'm longing to hear what happened. How did it begin?'

'I suppose,' said Sybil, 'it began with the grey cat. This cat seemed to come from nowhere. We caught sight of it one day in the garden. It was sitting on the terrace outside the french windows looking at us. It was a thin creature, but big. Grey all over, and with such smooth short fur that it looked from certain angles almost hairless. It had huge amber eyes that stared and stared. Miss Isabel was never a lover of cats, it's true, but she took against this one in a way that was a little . . .' Sybil paused, trying to find the right word, 'excessive. That's it. Excessive.

The first time she saw it, she sprang up from her seat on one of the garden benches and gave a cry of horror.

"'Oh, Sybil,'" she shivered. "Get rid of it. Please get rid of it."

'I stood up too, and began to say "shoo" and clap my hands in the general direction of the cat. It didn't move. It didn't flinch. I don't think it even blinked, but simply continued gazing at us with those enormous amber eyes. Then Miss Isabel did something quite unlike her. She was the calmest and gentlest of young ladies, and very dignified, but she knelt down and picked up two handfuls of gravel. Then she approached the cat and threw both handfuls of small stones straight at it as hard as she could throw. Her face was quite red from the effort, and she sat down on the garden bench again, shaking and trembling in every limb. The cat fled, of course, stung by the hail of tiny hard stones, but at the edge of the lawn he turned round, and fixing Miss Isabel with an unblinking gaze, he opened his mouth and hissed at her, showing sharp white teeth. Then he found a place in the shadow of a rhododendron, and sat there on his haunches, unmoving.

'He was always there after that. He never lay down. He never seemed to close his eyes. He never approached us, Miss Isabel and me, as we walked round the garden, but we felt him looking at us wherever we went. Miss Isabel couldn't bear it. After a while, she stopped walking in the garden altogether, but that didn't help. The cat came nearer and nearer to the house then, sometimes sitting right outside the french windows and staring in, and sometimes jumping up on to the outside windowsills, and pressing his nose against the glass, so that his breath misted the window. And then, one terrible day (oh, I'll never forget that day!) the cat found its way into the house, and into Miss Isabel's bedroom.

'The first I knew about it was the screaming. I was in the kitchen when I heard it, and I realized at once that it was Miss Isabel. I ran upstairs and the screams continued. It was like nothing else I've ever heard before or since, a noise like something tearing, or being torn apart. By the time I reached the bedroom door, it was already open and Miss Isabel's parents were there, comforting her, holding her, soothing her.

"'Fetch hot water, Sybil, quickly!" Mrs Winterthorne said to me. "And bandages. Run now."

'Miss Isabel's gown was torn. Her hands were covered in long, scarlet scratches dotted with drops of blood. Later, after she had calmed down, she told me, as well as she was able to, what had happened. The cat was on her bed. It wouldn't move. She clapped her hands at it. She flapped her shawl at it, but it stayed there as though it had grown roots that fastened it to the bedspread. Miss Isabel couldn't explain why she did what she did next. She went to pick up the cat, thinking to put it outside her door at least, but it began to struggle, and to claw at Miss Isabel's hands and the sleeves of her gown. She threw it away from her, not realizing how *frantic* she was, what unaccustomed strength was in her arms. The cat flew across the room, catching its back leg on the corner of the chest-of-drawers.

'"I think I hurt its leg," Miss Isabel told me. "It limped out of the room, dragging its leg behind it . . . oh, it was dreadful . . . and it looked at me with those terrible eyes as it went, and it was hissing. I can't bear it, Sybil, I can't bear it. What will I do if it comes back?"

'I told her it wouldn't come back, though of course I had no idea whether it would or not, but I had to calm her down, somehow. I had to cheer her up. I changed the subject. I began to talk about the following evening, when the Winterthornes were entertaining several local families to dinner and cards. Our conversation turned to dresses and hair ornaments, and slowly Miss Isabel became quieter. By the time I left her to go to my room in the attic, she was quite herself.'

'What about the cat?' Bridget asked. 'What happened to him?'

'We never laid eyes on him again. But the very next evening, Isabel met Captain Ashe and that was that.'

'What do you mean: that was that?'

'I mean,' said Sybil, 'that her fate was sealed from the moment she laid eyes on him. There was not a force in the universe that could have kept them apart.' Sybil held up her two hands and brought them together with the fingers intertwined and locked together. 'It was like watching something being drawn towards a magnet.' Sybil smiled. 'Captain Ashe was the most extraordinary-looking man: tall, slim, smooth with pale blond hair and strange yellowy-brown eyes. It was in my mind

as soon as I saw him that his eyes were just like those of the grey cat, but Miss Isabel clearly liked him, and I didn't think I should draw the resemblance to her attention.'

'Did you think he *was* the grey cat, changed in some mysterious way into a man? Come back to get his revenge on Isabel who had been so cruel to him?'

Sybil laughed. 'I *did* think that... but I quickly told myself off for being a silly ignorant girl. How could such things go on in a modern sort of world? But still, I had nightmares about Captain Ashe. In my dreams he had a limp. He was dragging his left foot behind him, only of course it wasn't a human foot at all, but a cat's paw sticking out of the khaki trouser leg ... oh, it gives me the shudders even now to think of it!'

'What happened then?'

'Well, Miss Isabel and Captain Ashe became engaged, and then married and we all thought that everything would be happy ever after, just like in the fairytales, but we had counted without the war. It had been decided that until the conflict was over, Miss Isabel (I couldn't help but keep calling her that, even though she wasn't a Miss any longer) should stay at home. We grew very close as the months passed. The captain was in France and every day that went by without us seeing his name on the casualty lists we counted as a happy one. Miss Isabel confided in me as we knitted socks for the troops ... how much she loved him ... how much she missed him. And ... you have to remember that in those days we were not so free and easy about sex in our conversation, as all you young people are. She never said so directly, of course, but I understood from all kinds of hints she dropped that ... well, that they were well-suited to one another. I shan't say more than that.

'Then, towards the end of 1916, the captain came home. He had been wounded. His left foot, just as I had dreamed it. The bandages were covered by a grey sock ... oh, I trembled when I saw him, limping across the hall, that first day. Miss Isabel's face when she caught sight of him would have done as a lamp, it was that happy.'

Sybil fell silent. She shook her head.

'Do go on,' said Bridget. 'What happened next?'

'The captain had changed. He was quiet and moody at first and then he stopped speaking altogether. This was bad enough of course, but we had all heard what the fighting did to the young men who had been in it, and we made allowances. It was decided that until the captain had quite recovered, he and Miss Isabel should continue to make Willow Grange their home. Mr and Mrs Winterthorne forgave him everything, but I was the one who helped Miss Isabel to dress and undress and I could forgive him nothing.

'"Don't say a word, Sybil," Miss Isabel begged me, seeing my eyes open at the bruises all over her lovely white skin. One day, I noticed scratches round her wrists, but I said nothing. In the end, after several weeks, Isabel spoke to her parents. There were lights burning in the study until very late at night, and the next day Captain Ashe left the house forever. I saw him limping down the drive, and at the gate he turned and looked straight up at Miss Isabel's window. Perhaps he thought I was Miss Isabel. In any case, he smiled and I saw his sharp white teeth and the yellow light shining out of his eyes.'

'So Isabel was happy after all . . .'

'Not for long. It soon became clear that she was expecting a baby.

'"How can I?" she used to say to me, and I would answer, "The child will remind you of better times. Of the days when you still loved the captain. After all, the baby won't have been changed by the war. It'll be the *real* Captain Ashe's child . . . will it be a boy or a girl, I wonder?"

'Over the months of her pregnancy, Miss Isabel grew gradually happier. We stopped knitting socks and turned our efforts to tiny garments. Then the baby was born, a lovely girl, with almond-shaped eyes of a colour that reminded everyone of her father, and a soft golden down on her head. She was a pretty little thing. I hadn't much experience of babies, but everyone said how unusual her eyes were, and how they weren't the dull blue of most newborn infants, and how they seemed to look right through you. Miss Isabel called her Elizabeth. Bessie.

'When Bessie was three days old, my own mother took sick, and I was sent for to go and nurse her. I was away for four days. As soon as I returned, even before I'd knocked at the door, I knew something terrible had happened. The curtains had been pulled across all the windows. Someone had died.

'"Is it Miss Isabel?" I asked Johnson, who opened the door to me.

'"No," he answered. "She's in her room. I doubt they'll let you see her. The doctor's been."

'"But why are all the curtains drawn? Who is dead?"

'"It's the baby. Little Bessie."

'I didn't wait to hear any more, but flew upstairs to be at Miss Isabel's side.

'When Mrs Winterthorne saw me, she said, "Oh, Sybil, my dear. Thank goodness you are here." Her eyes were scarlet with weeping. "Speak to her. Comfort her."

'I persuaded Mrs Winterthorne to go and lie down, now that I was here. When she had gone, I sat beside Miss Isabel. She was pale and looked tired, but seemed very calm.

'"Sybil," she said. "You will believe me, will you not?"

'"Yes, Miss Isabel."

'"Because I've never lied to you. They are coming tomorrow to take me to an Institution. You know what that means, Sybil. But at least my parents will not call the police. An empty coffin will be buried. I shall cheat the hangman."

'I burst into tears. I couldn't help it. The shock was too much.

'"Why?" I cried. "What has happened?"

'"I killed her," Miss Isabel said quietly. "I took her down to the lake and held her under the water until she was dead. I had to."

'"Why?" I asked. "Why did you have to?"

'Miss Isabel turned placid blue eyes upon me.

'"Because," she said clearly, "Bessie was turning into a cat. I heard her quite plainly, purring in her cot. The sound was almost deafening. Such things cannot be allowed to exist... such monstrosities. I had to drown her. I loved her, you see. You do see, don't you? No one else understands. I had to . . ."'

Sybil's voice faltered. She could hardly speak for crying.

'I'm so sorry,' said Bridget. 'I never meant the story to upset you. It's so sad. What happened after that?'

'Miss Isabel was sent abroad to a sanatorium. I was given my notice. The Winterthornes sold the house and left the area. I tried to put the whole thing out of my mind or I would have ended up in the madhouse as well. I never went near the house again, although over the years I've heard stories about it.

There's something crying in the night. It could be a baby, or perhaps a cat. No one stays long in the house though. Let's leave the paper now, dear, shall we? I'm not in the mood for news any longer. You can come and tell me the latest again next week.'

On the following Thursday, Bridget hurried to Holmecroft with the newspaper. She could scarcely wait to tell Sybil the news.

'I'm so terribly sorry, dear,' said the matron. 'Sybil passed away two days ago.'

'But she can't have,' Bridget burst out.

'She was ninety-three, dear,' said the matron. 'It was a long, happy life. She died very peacefully.'

'I wanted to . . .' Bridget started to say, and changed her mind. There was no point.

When she got home, she cut the small paragraph out of the newspaper, as a souvenir. She read it again.

KIND WORKMEN BURY OLD BONES

Last Friday morning, workmen busy on the site of the ornamental lake at Willow Grange came across the bones of what is thought to be a small cat. The police were called in, but gave permission for the remains to be disposed of.

'It looked so sad,' said foreman Mr Michael Raines, 'that we decided to bury it properly. We put all the bones we could find under a pink rhododendron bush, and said a few prayers. Perhaps it was a family pet that fell into the lake and got entangled in the waterlily roots or something. We all hope the poor little thing will rest in peace.'

Amen, thought Bridget. Amen.

Bewitched

JOHN GORDON

S he was a very pretty girl, no one denied that; and Tim
Spinks was very lucky she had chosen him. But Tim was
attracted by more than her good looks; in fact, they suited
each other so well that when, one day, he turned his back on her
so cruelly no one understood it, least of all the girl herself.

Tim and the girl—it would not be fair to give her name—had
a lot in common, and one thing in particular. They were
fascinated by things that flew—anything from airliners to hang
gliders, and even kites. They flew kites of all colours and sizes,
and at weekends you would see them on the downs gazing
skywards at the bright specks their kites made against the
clouds and you could not doubt that their hearts were up there
with them. And they had kites that could dance nearer the
ground; kites like birds, or dragons, or butterflies.

It was a kite like a gaudy butterfly that caused the trouble.

The girl had one she particularly loved and she could make it do the most fantastic imitations of a true butterfly, but one day, causing it to flutter too near a copse of tall trees, she caught it in the topmost branches and no tugging or manoeuvring could bring it down. It was ruined and far out of reach.

The girl's disappointment was greater than even Tim could have expected. For an instant she had the expression of a small child that had lost a doll, and this so affected Tim that he put his arms around her. She was never quite sure whether it was this gesture that made her, for just a moment, play up to him as if she was a spoilt little girl, but that was what she did.

He was still holding her when they heard a new thrashing in the branches above and a second kite came clumsily down through the leaves and hung on its snagged lines. Somewhere from far off they heard voices but they could not see the owners, and the kite swung just a few feet from the ground in the centre of a ring of trees.

The girl, her eyes large with unshed tears, gazed first at the kite and then at Tim.

'Get it for me,' she said.

'But it's not ours,' said Tim.

'Don't be a coward,' said the girl. 'Get it!'

He had already moved to obey when he glanced back. There was the hint of a smile on her beautiful face. He paused. She saw his own face turn pale, and she widened her smile and said, 'I shouldn't have said that . . . I didn't mean it.'

But it was too late. His eyes had hardened, and without a word he turned his back on her and walked away.

It was a cold day, but at that moment Tim Spinks had stepped into a day years before, when he was no more than eleven. It was a day when the summer sun was hot and he sat alone in an empty school playground.

The school day was over, and Tim, like a traveller in a desert, had picked out the one cool spot under the fig tree that spread over from the headmaster's garden. He sat on the ground with his back against the iron railing and his mind began to fill up with a thought that shamed him.

The ground was hard and he shifted uncomfortably. His friends had gone home and he should have been able to do the same, but today his father was late home from work, his mother was out for the day, and Tim had forgotten his key. So he had two hours to spare and nothing to do except think about what Angela Wise had said to him an hour ago when, chasing a paper aeroplane, he had run through a ring of girls playing a game.

'You might think that's clever, Tim Spinks, when nobody's going to hurt you—but you're no more than just a scaredy-cat when it comes to anything else.'

'Such as?' He did not like Angela Wise.

'You'll see!' Her voice was as sharp as the needle gleam in the black eyes she fixed on him. 'We'll cast a spell on you!'

A spell. He laughed at that because it told him what they were doing. They were playing at magic because someone had seen a fairy ring on the lawn of the headmaster's garden.

'Soppy fairy rings,' he said. 'You can't hurt me—words don't mean a thing.'

The girls, who a moment ago had been happy and laughing, were now sullen and angry, and shamefaced at having been caught out playing a game that was secret and now seemed babyish. But Angela Wise was not like the rest.

'You'll be sorry,' she said. 'I know someone.'

'I don't care who you know. He can't scare me.'

'Who said anything about a He?'

'I'm not afraid of any girl,' said Tim.

'Who said it was a girl?' The trouble with Angela Wise was not just that she was dark and secretive; she could also steal boys' hearts, and knew it. She tossed her hair and lifted her chin. 'Did I *say* it was a girl?'

'It's your mother, then.'

'Why should I tell you anything?' She turned away.

Not many people could say where Angela Wise lived, but Tim knew because he had once seen her in the clump of crumbling little houses close to the print works where his father was a printer. It was not a street he had ever walked down, but he had once been at the works with his father and had seen Angela turning the corner of the street. She was with a woman who was small and grey-haired but whose face was made up to look like someone so much younger that one of his father's friends had muttered something which had made both men laugh.

'I know your mother,' he said to Angela's back. 'She's nothing to be afraid of. She's too old.'

He knew as he said it that he should never have been so cruel, but a moment later Angela had picked up his paper aeroplane and torn it in two, which had made him too angry to apologize. And now, alone in the hot afternoon, he could not keep Angela Wise out of his mind. The spell was nothing, but she had taunted him with being a coward. Was he? Was breaking up a girls' game the only brave thing he dared do?

He suddenly found himself sweating, and it wasn't the heat. He knew what was about to happen. He was going to have to dare himself to do something to prove himself, and lonely dares were the worst. They were the ones that mattered.

He looked across at the high wall that separated the playground from the road outside and thought of climbing up and walking along it. But he'd already done that, with his eyes closed, and everybody had seen him, which made it easier. If he wanted a real test he would have to trespass in the headmaster's garden with nobody watching. Mr Morris was fierce with anybody who even took one of the green figs that overhung the playground, and what he would do to someone he caught creeping through his bushes didn't bear thinking about . . . even if you told him you were only trying to see if there really was a fairy ring on the lawn. But that was what Tim knew he had to do. Alone and right now.

'It wouldn't be so bad,' he said aloud, 'if there was someone else around.'

It was then that he heard a sound. It came from the shrubbery on the other side of the railing at his back and it made him jump. It was no more than the sound a startled bird would make flapping among the leaves, but then came a quick patter of feet like a running dog that made him start to his feet and spin around.

But no dog was charging towards him and no bird flew out screeching in alarm. What he saw was beyond the dark banks of shrubbery in the sunlight on the headmaster's lawn. It was a girl, and she appeared to be dancing. He was suspicious of that. Girls who danced alone with long hair flowing free and raising their faces to the sky as they gracefully lifted their arms were best avoided. They always behaved as though they were saying something wonderfully special, when everyone else knew that words would have been much better.

He was about to turn away when he saw that this girl was not dancing. Her gracefulness was simply the way she ran as she tried to catch something that fluttered over her head. It was a bright bird and, although it flew very clumsily, it just escaped her fingers and flapped into the bushes.

The girl stooped and was hidden by the thick leaves. Tim could not see what she did. The bird must have been injured to fly so badly, but there had been something in the girl's expression that made Tim wonder, in spite of her prettiness, whether she was chasing it to comfort it or whether she was hunting and wanted to kill it. She had hair as tawny as a lion and grey slanting eyes.

Then she stood up, with her back towards him, and released something from her hands. But it was not a bird. It was—there could be no doubt about it—a butterfly, but an impossible one. It was as big as a bird, and its bright wings spread out like two small hands that beat the air with such a clash of colours they seemed to clatter, and it did not fly well. It staggered in the air, turning back towards the bushes, and its stiff wings were soon battering the leaves once more.

The girl had spun around to follow it, but as she did so she caught sight of Tim in the playground and suddenly stood still. Her face was as small-nosed and large-eyed as a cat's, and like a cat she gazed at him without blinking.

Tim was embarrassed. He had been caught peeping, and he opened his mouth to say sorry, but before he could speak she smiled. He had never seen a face so pretty or a smile that troubled him so much. It teased him so slyly that he dipped his head to hide his face and raised his hand to say farewell.

He was turning away when, from the corner of his eye, he saw that she had raised her hand in exactly the same way and even mimicked his dipped head and solemn face. She was making fun of him. He put out his tongue. She did the same, except that she licked her upper lip with a flick as quick as a lizard's. She was insulting him and tempting him at the same time. Then she spoke. 'I think you are a coward,' she said.

'No, I'm not!' His cheeks were hot. 'Why am I?'

'Because you are, and you know you are.'

He glowered at her. 'You wouldn't dare say that if you were someone else!'

'You mean if I was a boy?' She lowered her eyelids over her large grey eyes, and then raised them. The way she did it was enough to prove she was no boy, but she said it nevertheless. 'And I'm not a boy, am I?'

She did not bother to listen for a reply, but immediately lost interest in him and stooped to disentangle the flying creature's wings from the bush. It was then that he saw that the wings were not soft and powdery as they should have been, but scraped harshly on the twigs, and a moment later it was obvious that it was not a living creature at all. It was a paper butterfly, which interested him even more, but when she had freed it she held it behind her back.

'You want to see it, don't you?' She seemed to read his mind very easily. 'But you're scared to come any closer because little boys get into trouble if the headmaster catches them in his garden.'

He couldn't let her get away with that, so he gripped the top rail of the fence and vaulted over. A moment later he had pushed through the shrubbery and stood with the girl at the edge of the lawn. He did not look directly at her but kept his eyes on the house where, in the dark rooms behind the glint of the windows, angry eyes may be on him at that moment.

'No need to look so worried,' she said. 'No one is watching.'

'I don't care if there is.' She said nothing, but her lips made a small O and her eyes were wide as if she was mocking him again, so he added, 'I often come over here—whenever I feel like it.' It was a lie.

'So,' she said, and her voice was so quiet he had to lean towards her, 'you have been watching me all the time. Why did you do that, Tim Spinks?' She was gazing down at her toes as if she was ashamed at what she may have done and what he may have seen.

'I didn't mean to,' he blurted out. 'I just couldn't help it!' And that suddenly sounded as if he couldn't help spying on her because he thought she was pretty, and she looked up.

'Why are you blushing, Tim Spinks?'

She was making him feel awkward again, and he spoke roughly to break free. 'What are you doing here, anyway? Do you live here, or something?'

'Me?' She was laughing. 'Has the headmaster suddenly got a daughter? If I lived here you'd have seen me a long time ago.'

'Well what are you doing here if this isn't your garden?'

'It's my garden if I say so.' She tilted her head to gaze up at the tops of the trees. Every time she moved he saw something new in her. This time it was that her nostrils were so small and perfect that, for a moment, he wondered if she had to do anything so commonplace as to breathe in order to live. He forced himself to challenge her once more.

'You are just making everything up as you go along,' he said. 'You'll be pretending to be a witch in a minute, or a fairy or something else stupid.'

'If I was a witch,' the girl said, 'I wouldn't have to bother to turn you into a toad because you look like one already.'

He knew he should not have taken her seriously, but he could not stop himself saying, 'Why did you say that? I haven't done anything to you.'

'And you haven't done anything *for* me, either.'

'Why should I?'

'You said I was a witch, so I may be able to grant you a wish.'

'You can't do anything.'

'Oh, can't I?' Her smile was conceited. 'I've already granted one thing you wished for.'

'And what's that?' He was scornful.

'When you were sitting in the playground you wished you weren't alone—and here I am.'

'You heard me say that. You were in the bushes all the time.'

'Was I? I thought I was out here on the lawn.' She shrugged. 'Anyway, even if you don't think that's your first wish, I can certainly grant your second.'

'Oh, can you?' He tried to put a sneer in his voice. 'I suppose you can grant it even if you don't know what it is.'

'Oh, but I do know what it is. You wish you could see what it is I've got behind my back.'

That was not a real wish, but she had got the better of him again. He badly wanted to see the paper butterfly, but he was not going to say so.

'I'll show you,' she said, 'if you make me a promise.'

'No.' He was determined. 'I want to see it first, and then I might promise.'

'Very well.' She brought her hand from behind her back, and laid the butterfly on his palm. In spite of its size it looked real. Its delicate wings even quivered as though at any moment they would beat the air and it would lift from his fingers.

'How do I wind it up?' he asked. There had to be an elastic band somewhere, and he was about to turn the butterfly over to examine its mechanism when she interrupted him.

'Can't you see it's broken?' she said. 'Look at its wing.' She spread the wing out and he saw that the brightly coloured paper had a jagged tear across it. 'And it's all your fault, Tim Spinks. It would never have crashed into the bushes if you hadn't been spying on me.'

That was the third time she'd proved she knew him, but he had no idea who she was. 'What's your name?' he asked.

'Never mind about that—you made me a promise.'

He was suspicious. 'What do you want me to do?'

'It's not very much.' Her voice became soft and wheedling, as if she was going to ask him to perform some heroic deed. 'I want a new butterfly.'

He was disappointed. 'Is that all?' he said.

'Tim,' she said, with her large eyes on him, 'I shall get into terrible trouble for breaking this one.'

'Well, just tell me where you got it and I'll go there straight away.'

'You're very kind,' she said. 'But you'll have to buy a comic—it's that new one called *Antics*. The butterfly was a free gift.'

He had never heard of *Antics* and he had seen no one with a paper butterfly. He did not know where to go.

'There's only one place I've ever seen it,' she said. 'It's a tiny little shop.'

'Come with me and show me.'

'No, I can't. I've got to stay here.'

'Why?'

'I just can't go, that's all.' She gazed at the ground and then slowly swung her head as if her eyes were following some invisible trail. Her gaze was so intense that he also looked down, and then he, too, saw what it was. Toadstools had made a fairy ring and she was standing in the middle of it. 'I can't leave,' she said quietly. 'It's bad luck.'

It made him smile to see that she was playing the girls' game with the fairy ring. 'All right,' he said, 'I'll go alone.'

'It's that little shop on the other side of the park . . . you know, the one called *Near As Can Do*.'

Tim laughed because he had heard the name before. His mother and father had talked about the shop they used to know years ago, when they were at school. He had never heard anyone else mention *Near As Can Do*, but he did know how it got its name. The old man who kept it never seemed to have what you needed and he always came up with something else which was 'as near as can do'. Tim had always thought the shop must have been pulled down long ago, but now the girl had told him where it was.

'You'll have to hurry,' she said. 'It's getting late.'

'I'll run.'

'I'll be ever so grateful.' Her smile made him so eager to do what she asked that he had already taken two steps before a sudden thought struck him and he pulled up.

'I haven't any money,' he admitted. His key was not the only thing he'd forgotten that morning. 'And I can't get any.'

'Nor can I. Witches don't have pockets.' She pulled at her skirt to show him.

He looked towards the headmaster's house, but she saw what he was thinking and she shook her head. 'I don't belong there,' she said. 'I'm a long way from home.'

He had let her down. 'I'm sorry,' he said. 'There's nothing I can do.'

'Yes, there is.'

Her reply came so swiftly that he was startled. And her eyes were on him, full of meaning. It was a full two seconds before he guessed what was in her mind. She did not care what he did to get the butterfly, whether he paid for it or not.

'No.' He shook his head. 'I can't do that.'

'Yes you can.'

'It's stealing.'

'But I've *got* to have it!' she said. 'It means so much to me.' Her eyes held his, and he could not look away. He knew he was going to do whatever she asked and his heart began to thud heavily, but before he could say anything she lowered her eyelids and spoke so softly and quickly that he had to lean forward. 'I'll be nice to you when you get back,' she said. 'I'll . . .' and then her voice dropped away completely.

'I didn't hear you!'

This made her laugh at him. 'I'll be hiding in the bushes when you get back—and then you'll see. Now go quickly.'

It was late in the afternoon and the park was almost empty. The shop, she had told him, was at the far corner, and it would soon be closed. He ran across the grass, panting in the heat but glad to be doing something energetic to take his mind off what he had promised to do when he got there.

As his feet pounded the turf, however, he realized he was heading into a part of the park he hardly knew. It was cut off by bowling pavilions and hedges from the open spaces where he flew his kite, and it had always seemed too dull to explore. But there was a small gate that he had never paid much attention to, and he went through to find himself in a narrow roadway wedged between the high hedge of the park and the blank wall of a large building.

It was dusty and very quiet except for the hum of machinery from the other side of the wall and it dawned on him that he was behind the printing works. It was only later that he realized he could have had the money for the comic by simply going into the works and asking to see his father, but he had never been in this narrow road before, and his father seemed far away.

The road curved away to his right until it disappeared behind a bend, and to his left it was cut off by a row of posts to keep cars out. But where was the shop?

Beyond the posts there was a glimpse of houses, and he ran towards them, panicking at the thought he may be going in the wrong direction, but suddenly the hedge on his left came to an end, and there it was.

It was very small for a shop, like one of the black wooden pavilions alongside the bowling green, and it stood back from the road in a patch of gravel overshadowed by the tall park trees. Its single square window was stacked with cartons, and an ice-cream sign stood outside so he knew it was not yet closed. Its open doorway was behind a curtain of brightly painted beads to keep out the flies. He lifted them aside and went in.

The floor was of black and red tiles, but so many shelves and stacks of boxes crowded around him that Tim felt he could not

move from the square on which he stood without knocking
something over. The counter had a row of huge glass bottles full
of sweets, with just enough space between them for him to see
a door behind it leading to a room where the shopkeeper lived.
But there was no one in the shop, and it was warm and stuffy
and very quiet.

He had come through the door with some idea in his mind
that he would be able to hide behind other customers and pick
up the comic without being seen, but the deserted shop seemed
to be asking him to help himself.

There was a shelf of newspapers and magazines. He found
the comics and began to go through them, muttering over and
over again *I'll pay tomorrow, I'll pay tomorrow* as if that would
protect him if he was caught. But he could not find what he was
looking for. The girl was wrong; there was no comic called
Antics and no free gift, and suddenly he had nothing to worry
about.

He let out his breath in relief, and he was still stooping over
the shelf when a soft, smothered thud behind him made him
spin around. Something the size of a pillow seemed to have
fallen on the counter, and was humped among the sweet bottles.
From the centre of the hump a pair of eyes peered at him
through the dimness. For a moment it seemed to be a single,
monstrous furry head, but then he saw what it was. A cat,
which seemed bigger than any he had seen before, had jumped
on to the counter, and crouched there, among the bottles,
grumbling in its throat as it purred.

Tim backed away. The cat was large, but there was no need
to be afraid. He had almost reached the door when, with a leap
in his throat, the panic returned. Just beneath the cat's
haunches, under its waving tail, a comic lay on the counter. He
could see its name, *Antics*, and the announcement in big splashy
print: Free Gift Inside! And there was a picture of a dazzling
butterfly.

He went forward. The cat watched but did not budge. His
hand reached *Antics*. He held its edge and was beginning to ease
it out, keeping his gaze fixed on the cat's grey and amber eyes,
when its tail flicked suddenly at his wrist and made him jerk
back. The movement was too sharp. He held on to the comic
but its pages spilled open and the butterfly fell out. It should

have reached the floor, but instead of that its wings began to beat and it rose, fluttering towards the ceiling.

And it was worse than that. The cat sprang from the counter and as it did so it barged into a tall bottle of sweets and sent it plunging to the floor. It hit the tiles and smashed. A cascade of amber sweets spread out as the butterfly, exhausted with battering at the ceiling, fell among them. Tim stooped, grabbed it among a handful of sweets, and scrambled towards the open air.

The strings of beads clung to his hair and neck and made him stagger as he forced his way through the doorway and he stumbled and fell to the gravel on all fours.

But he was out in the open, and he had the butterfly in his hand. All he had to do was run. He was pushing himself to his feet when something gripped his shoulder. He twisted, and the grip got tighter. It hurt.

'What's the big hurry, son?' The man who held him was white-haired but his hand was strong.

Tim's mouth opened, but no words came.

'In there, were you?' The man dipped his head towards the shop. Tim nodded, and the man looked sternly down at him for a long time until gradually the wrinkles in his face changed slightly and he seemed to be smiling. 'Get what you wanted, did you?' he asked.

'I was going to pay,' said Tim.

'Going to pay?' The man was amused. 'I wonder what it was you bought in there.' Once more he nodded towards the shop and this time he allowed Tim to turn around and face it. 'They don't have much for sale in that old place nowadays.'

The man chuckled, but Tim did not hear him. He was gazing at the shop. It was not the same. A few black boards remained upright but the roof had fallen in, and the doorway gaped on nothingness with a few straggles of honeysuckle where the bead curtain had been.

'So you got what you wanted, did you, son?'

'I think so.'

'Well, that'll be the first time anybody ever did,' said the man. 'Old *Near As Can Do* never had anything I asked for.'

Tim looked up at the man. 'But I was in there,' he said, 'and there was a cat sitting on the counter.'

'Was there?' The man's smile broadened. 'In my day it was a girl. Old *Near As Can Do* had a granddaughter and she was always sitting on the counter.'

'No, it was a cat,' Tim insisted. 'And it knocked a bottle of sweets on the floor, and I've got some.' He opened his fingers. He had a fistful of pebbles, and there was no butterfly.

The man laughed again. 'You've got quite an imagination, boy. In my day it was the girl who got us into trouble. Every time one of us lads went in she'd look at us with those eyes of hers then call out to old *Near As Can Do* that we were trying to nick things off the shelves. Got no end of boys into a real scrape, she did; just as if she hated every one of us. But she was pretty, all right, and I'll never forget those great big beautiful eyes of hers . . . !' He shook his head. 'She was a wicked little witch, that one.'

The man thought for a moment and then he gave Tim's shoulder a push. 'Off you go, boy, and don't let me ever catch you playing about in there again—it can be dangerous.'

It was hot walking back across the park, and hotter still in the school playground. But it was quiet there. He would tell the girl everything that had happened and she would believe him, even if nobody else ever did.

He climbed the railing into the headmaster's garden and began to push his way through the bushes. The girl had not told him her name so he called out 'Are you there?' as he went. There was no reply.

At the edge of the lawn he saw the toadstool ring and he called again. There was still no answer, but within the ring something moved. He saw what it was. Her paper butterfly lay on the grass, and its torn wing was lifted by a faint breeze. He went to it and was about to pick it up when, from the house, a voice roared angrily at him: 'If I catch you, you'll be for it!'

He turned and bolted into the shrubbery like a rabbit. Twigs lashed his face and tore at his clothes but he reached the railing and scrambled over.

Panting, he paused to listen. He was never sure if anyone had followed him, but he was certain that, somewhere among the trees, a girl was laughing. He turned his back and ran.

The Flying Dustman

MICK GOWAR

Message received by Space Station Senta on 13.7.2020. Message received on Formaldehyde frequency. Rebroadcast to DRB, Earth, 14.7.2020.

Hullo . . . Hullo . . . Hullo . . . Can anyone hear me? Hullo . . . Hullo . . . If anyone can hear me, please record this message and pass it on to Debris Reclamation Base. Tell them I haven't done a bunk. Tell them I'm still alive—but I don't know for how much longer.

I would ask for help, but I can't give you my position. Through the ports, all I can see is blackness, complete blackness. No stars—nothing. At first I thought it was a gas cloud . . . but it's been too long. Five days of total darkness.

According to the instruments, my life support systems packed up two days ago. But I'm still alive—aren't I?

Sorry. That's a lousy way to start a report. I'll try and do it properly.

My name is Spencer, Stan Spencer. Occupation: Debris Reclamation Patrol—or, as you probably know it, Junk Jockey. Flying Dustman. The lowest of the low. Stuck out in Earth orbit picking up bits of crocked satellite, discarded junk from Space Stations, and, of course, everybody's favourite—jettisoned hygiene units from Spaceliners. Like they say: it's a crappy job but someone's got to do it!

Don't get me wrong, there are compensations. It's a job, and that's something for a bloke like me with a Gamma-Minus education. And you do get your own spacecraft, even if it is only a clapped-out Scud with a couple of hydraulic grabbers underneath. But best of all, there's no boss breathing down the back of your neck. Sure, there's radio contact with Base, but I only use that if I hit a *real* problem; and Base don't usually bother to contact me. Not boasting, but I'm a good worker, and they leave me pretty much alone.

That's OK with me. I don't mind being on my own. It's only blokes who think too much who have problems being on their own up here. And I've never been much of a thinker—come to that, what Junk Jockey ever was? So I've never felt lonely . . . not until now.

It's nearly a week since I caught that *thing* in the grabbers. Boy! Was it ever a weirdo! None of the sensors registered. I went through all the usual tests, *twice*, but the answer kept coming out the same: 'No known substance.' And that's a real problem, because I didn't know which storage bin to put it in. You can't risk contamination; contaminate a storage bin and bang goes your bonus.

Anyway, the visuals were on the blink again, so I couldn't even see what it was I'd got.

I called Base: 'Permission to jettison.'

The answer came back: 'Permission denied. Proceed with further examination.'

So I said, 'What do you mean, *proceed*? I've done all the tests: "No known substance", and the visuals have packed up again.'

But they weren't having any of it. 'Permission to jettison denied. Dismantle, and proceed with structural analysis.'

Easy for them to say! They should try taking a dirty great

lump of space junk to pieces with a pair of clumsy great grabbers and no visuals!

Just then, something really weird happened. Something came through on the audio. It sounded like a cry—like someone or something in pain.

I should have mentioned, there's an audio link to the outside of the ship for when we're in port doing ground maintenance. Of course, it's useless in space. There's no air up here, just a vacuum; and everybody knows you can't have sound in a vacuum. So when I heard the noise, I thought: Oh no! Now the audio's on the blink, too!

So I tightened the grabbers ready to start dismantling—as I'd been told to—and it happened again; a shriek, like something in pain. Creepy, but like I said: no air, no sound—right? Nothing can shriek in space.

I reported back to Base again. 'Visuals down and audio malfunctioning. Permission to jettison.'

Back came the same reply: 'Permission denied. Proceed with dismantling and analysis.' Just what you need at the end of a long shift!

The noise was still coming through, so I turned the volume right down. But—and this was the weirdest thing—even with the volume on the audio turned down to '0' the noise was still coming through as loud as ever, but this time it was a sort of regular sobbing. But I knew it had to be static, or feedback, or something like that. It couldn't have been the thing in the grabbers. Garbage can't sob; garbage can't feel pain.

So I started the dismantling procedure. It's not a difficult operation, really; you just pull the grabbers apart and see what's inside—except I couldn't see, so I had to rely on the sensors.

I pulled the grabbers apart. *Jesus!* You should have heard it! The audio went bonkers. Scream, after scream, after scream! Honestly, that's just what it sounded like. Only, I knew it couldn't be. No air, no sound—right? Nothing can scream in space. Except, I could hear it; I could hear screaming.

By this time I was starting to get seriously spooked, so I thumped the control panel just by the audio switches. It didn't stop the screaming, but that thump must have done something to the visuals. The screen flickered, then filled with grey specks, then slowly cleared.

And then there was more screaming—but this time it was me, screaming at what I could see on the screen. Screaming at the sight of the thing I'd caught in the grabbers.

In the claw of one of the grabbers was what looked like a huge pair of wings, and in the other was a body. It was a man's body . . . well, except for the colour; it was a metallic, sort of gold colour. It was dead.

Then, without so much as a warning flicker, the screen went dead again. I rushed to the side port, to see if I could get just a glimpse of the thing in the grabbers. But outside, everything was dark—everything, pitch black; no stars, no planets. Nothing.

At first I thought I must have got into a gas cloud . . . but it's been five days now, and everything is still pitch black. A black hole? No. I would have been squeezed out like a lump of spaghetti by now, and I haven't been.

In fact, physically I feel great, terrific. I haven't felt tired or thirsty or hungry for five days. Not since that thing got caught in the grabbers; not since the darkness came.

I've double checked the instruments; there must be some mistake, but I can't find one. According to the instruments the life support systems were exhausted two days ago. According to the instruments I should have died two days ago. But I didn't. I'm still alive; still travelling through this blackness without sleep or food or water.

Five days I've been travelling like this. I could go on for days, for weeks, for months, for years . . . I could go on like this forever.

It wasn't my fault! I didn't know what was in the grabbers! I didn't mean to kill it! I'm just a simple Junk Jockey; a Flying Dustman. It wasn't my fault!

I feel so frightened, so alone I could cry, shriek, scream . . . But it wouldn't do any good. There's nothing up here, just a vacuum. No air, no sound—right. I could cry, shriek, scream—but no one would ever hear me. No one would ever hear me . . .

Message Ends.

The Intake

GRACE HALLWORTH

Constable St Clair had been stationed at a country outpost for just a year when he received orders to patrol the first six miles of mountain road leading up to a place where the river was dammed. This place was known locally as 'The Intake' and from there water was piped to the villages scattered along the sides of the mountain.

The Intake was an eerie place even in daytime. About a mile off the road, it was heavily shrouded with large trees. Long thick vines wove themselves around massive tree trunks, binding the trees together and creating a lattice-work screen and support for climbing plants, snakes and birds. It was also the haunt of Les Diablesses and the villagers gave the place a wide berth at night.

At ten-thirty that evening St Clair left the station with a heavy heart, for he knew well the reputation of The Intake.

St Clair was no hero but he wanted to keep his record clean. And like everyone else in the police force he had his eye on quick promotion. Also, he knew that the superintendent was not above checking up on his men during the night patrol.

'Somehow or the other,' he argued with himself. 'I have to keep one eye out for the Super and the other eye out for Les Diablesses.'

St Clair arrived at the beginning of the mountain road and looked up as far as he could see. The moon shone brightly down on the road but off to the sides the trees grew thick and tall and it was impossible to see what lurked behind them. Back and forth, forth and back went the silent arguments in St Clair's head. Finally he said loud enough for any one who was nearby to hear, 'It's no use tempting fate and looking for trouble. If the Super come, well he come, but I don't intend going anywhere near that Intake tonight.' And having made his decision, he set out to patrol the road up to the three-mile post and not a foot further.

As he was climbing the road he heard voices. He stopped and listened carefully. From a distance they sounded like women's voices but he couldn't be sure. So he stood where he was and waited to see who would appear. He reached into his coat pocket for his torch, but there was so much light from the moon that it seemed pointless to turn it on.

As the voices came closer St Clair saw that they belonged to two young women. They were as pretty as money and St Clair was heartened by the presence of such beauty to enliven his night patrol. He greeted them with his unique brand of sweet talk, 'Goodnight, fair ladies. Will you allow a lonely policeman to join your delightful company and see you home?'

The young women laughed merrily at his manner of speech and one of them said, 'You don't even know where we live, yet you so eager to see us home!'

'Ah, but your home can't be very far away or such lovely young ladies would not be out so late?' rejoined St Clair.

'You are right, Mr St Clair,' said the other lady. 'We live just a little way from here and we welcome your protection. Who knows what we might meet on the way.'

St Clair was quite taken aback when he heard her call his name for he did not recognize either of the women, and he had not mentioned his name. But he supposed that he was well-known in the district. Besides he could not see their faces clearly and could not be sure that he had not spoken to one of them on some previous occasion. So he let it pass.

'Tell me,' he asked them, 'how far away do you live?'

'Just over a mile,' replied the one who had called him by name.

As they walked along St Clair wondered if his eyes were deceiving him. No matter how quickly he walked he could not catch up with those ladies and yet they did not appear to be walking fast. He began to feel uneasy. He noticed little things which he had missed when he first began to escort them. He could not hear the sound of their shoes on the road. In fact he could not tell whether they wore shoes, for their feet were hidden by long dresses. He was about to get his torch out when one of them said to him, 'We are nearly home, Mr St Clair. Will you take our hands and help us down?'

St Clair looked and saw that she was pointing in the direction of The Intake. She held out her hand to take his but instead of taking her arm, he took out his torch and shone the beam of light right on her.

He only managed to catch a glimpse of her face before the two women screamed and fled away from the piercing light of the torch. In a moment they were swallowed up in the forest of trees which were so close together that not even the moon's bright light could penetrate the darkness. Terror-stricken, St Clair fled down the mountain to the safety and bright lights of the main road.

When St Clair reported the incident to his superintendent he said, 'Nonsense, St Clair. A big man like you allow yourself to be fooled by two young ladies out to tease you! Man, you should be ashamed of yourself.'

But St Clair says he knows what he knows and the Super can say what he likes; no one is getting St Clair to patrol that road again. For when he looked into the face of the lady nearest him he saw two empty sockets where there should have been eyes!

Dog on Board

DENNIS HAMLEY

Amy was having a nightmare.

What a pity. Tomorrow morning the family was to get up early. The elderly D registered Range Rover, Dad's latest pride and joy, stood on the drive, already loaded up. The trailer tent was hitched on behind. After a quick breakfast, they would drive off two hundred miles to the camping site by the sea in Cornwall. Amy very seldom had bad dreams. But tonight, a puzzling inferno had started up in her mind.

How had the dream started? Amy didn't know. But Mum and Dad, elder brother and sister Mark and Rebecca were in it. So was Goldie, the retriever, who licked her with his rough tongue and looked at her through deep, liquid brown eyes. She remembered this even when the details of the dream were forgotten.

But now there was screeching and rending of metal, scorching heat and a wall of orange flame coming fast towards her. Mum and Dad were in front, Mark and Rebecca beside her. Their eyes were open and fixed: blood was everywhere. Goldie lay across her, heavy and warm, but also still: she knew he would never move again. She tried to move but something held her legs. And the flame came nearer and the heat got worse and worse . . .

She woke up. She was still hot. Her forehead was beaded with sweat, her nightie was drenched with it. But she was not alone. Something started licking her forehead and making it cooler.

Goldie. 'I've had a nasty dream,' she said to him. She knew that if it were not so dark, his brown eyes would gaze at her softly and understandingly.

She sat up. The air struck cold on her skin as it touched the sweat and made her shiver. There were shadows in the room which had not been there for years, since she was *very* little.

'Mummy,' she called.

The landing light went on. Mummy came in, switched on the little light which was kept just out of Amy's reach so she couldn't have it on all night, and said, 'What are you doing here, Goldie? Your place is downstairs.'

Goldie did not want to go. Mum led him away by the collar. But all the while Amy could still see him, he was looking back, watching her with those deep brown eyes. When he could see her no more and Mum had let his collar go, he gave a little whimper as if to say, 'Why can we dogs never make you humans understand?' Then he trotted downstairs.

'I wanted him to stay, Mummy,' said Amy.

'He's too clever by half, that dog. Especially now he's learnt to open all the doors himself.'

She bent over Amy. 'What's the matter, love?'

'I . . . I had a bad dream.'

Mum looked at her, placed a hand on her forehead, then said, 'I won't be a minute.'

Amy heard her voice in the next room. 'I don't like the look of her. She's running with sweat. It looks like she's got a fever.'

'She'll be OK.' Dad's voice was muffled under the duvet cover. 'Let her sweat it out. I'm not delaying the start of our holiday.'

Mum came back. She carried the little thermometer and

slipped it in Amy's mouth. A minute later she took it out, looked at it, said, relieved, 'Normal,' then bent over Amy again. 'Go to sleep, Amy. The bad dream's gone. Remember, we're getting up early tomorrow.'

How could she forget?

She closed her eyes. Sleep came at once—and with it, like a loaded trap waiting on her pillow, the same noise, blood, motionless bodies with sightless eyes and the approaching, searing, roaring flame . . .

Downstairs, in his basket, Goldie slept too. But now he jerked his legs and whimpered. Who could know what was going through his canine mind? Perhaps, now he had not been allowed to stay with Amy, something there was ranging far away, searching out someone else who might understand his message.

The motorway leading westward was thick with early morning fog. Now and again it lifted in deceptive clear patches, so cars and lorries delightedly increased speed. Then it would drop again, thicker than ever. If the fog could speak it would be laughing humourlessly. Some cars slowed at once, suddenly, hazard lights blinking like frightened eyes. Others had drivers who said, 'This doesn't apply to me. It will lift in a minute.' They carried on down the outside lane as if the sun shone from a clear sky.

Arthur Rowntree gripped the big steering wheel of his tanker lorry and peered forward. This, of all weathers, he hated most on the motorway. It didn't matter how careful he was: there were always idiots surrounding him. All right, his tanker was always excellently maintained. Arthur was a stickler for that. He wouldn't drive for a firm which didn't look after its vehicles properly. And this firm, Retro-Cychem PLC, positively had to. Ferrying dangerous chemicals from one end of the country to the other was no joke. Arthur didn't know the precise properties of whatever was sloshing about in the tank on the back. But he knew what he had to do if there was ever a leak— and it frightened him. He never dared think about a full-blown crash. But this morning the unthinkable had been nudging the back of his mind. He had woken in the small hours, sweating about it. He'd nearly rung the depot, said he was sick . . .

But Arthur Rowntree was a rational man. Risk and danger were, after all, part of life. If a few doubtful thoughts in the morning were to stop him earning his living . . .

Even so . . .

He made up his mind. Next services, he'd stop. A mug of tea, a bacon sandwich, and wait for this lot to go.

He was driving through a clear patch now. Blue showed through the white shroud overhead: the sun would break through in the end.

Then, without warning, the fog dropped on him again, worse than ever. Hazards on, drop speed—slow enough already. Hope that the airbrakes—which even at their best had longer stopping distances than cars—wouldn't meet something stuck in front that they couldn't cope with. No, they wouldn't . . . they wouldn't . . . would they?

Without warning, he saw it. Right below his cab, impossible not to hit, smash right into, destroy completely. No hazards on, just slogging along, painfully slowly: a dark green Range Rover pulling a trailer tent. D registration.

So clearly, etched in horribly sharp detail. The black cover strapped over the tent. The loaded roof-rack. The rear window. Stickers on it. Words burned for ever on his mind.

> CHILDREN ON BOARD • DOG ON BOARD
> A DOG IS FOR LIFE NOT JUST FOR CHRISTMAS

Across the bottom of the window, white lettering on blue:

> DAN, DAN, THE OFF-ROADER MAN
> ALL MAKES OF FOUR-WHEEL DRIVE VEHICLES:
> SALES AND SERVICE

The dog on board looked at him through the window. A beautiful golden retriever with deep, soulful, brown eyes. Driver and dog looked at each other: what message passed? Arthur didn't know, but he felt a well of unutterable sadness before the certain impact. For beyond the dog were three children. Beyond them . . .

And this would be their last moment on Earth. Because nothing could stop him . . .

Despairingly, he slammed on his brakes. Even in that split second, the consequences flooded into his mind. Would what was behind him go straight into the back of his tanker? What about the appalling liquid he carried? What if his tanker were thrown on its side, the tank breached, the contents spilled out— then the poison, the spreading death?

He found himself shouting at the top of his voice: 'I'm sorry. I'm *so* sorry. I didn't mean it.'

He kept his eyes open intently as he waited for the catastrophe.

'Amy's better,' said Mum. 'But I still don't like the look of her.'

Dad was tapping his foot impatiently. Mark and Rebecca were out, taking Goldie for one last walk before the journey. He sighed for the early hours, while the streets were still quiet and only the milkman disturbed the peace.

'I didn't want to have to wait,' he said. 'I wanted to beat the traffic around the town.'

Mum didn't tell her husband that Amy had cried and said she didn't want to go.

'I'll get the traffic reports,' said Dad and switched the radio on.

Fog on the M4. Dangerous driving conditions.

'I still want to beat the traffic,' said Dad.

Mum certainly didn't tell how Amy had cowered away when she had said, 'Come on, love, you're all right now. Get out of bed. We're off for our holiday.' The panic that was in her youngest child's eyes troubled her deeply.

The tanker lorry slid to a halt. For a moment, Arthur Rowntree sat in his cab, head bowed over the steering wheel, unable to look up. Then he forced himself.

His tanker had come to rest safely, two metres behind a stationary lorry. TRELAWNEY TRANSPORT SERVING CORNWALL was emblazoned on the back.

He jumped down from the cab and walked round the tanker. All seemed OK. Behind him was a black Ford Mondeo, headlights and hazards on.

Where was the Range Rover? He stepped on to the hard shoulder. Perhaps it had miraculously sheered off to avoid him.

He could not see more than five metres either way. He leaned up against the side of his cab. Relief flooded through him. His premonitions had not been fulfilled. He was safe—and so was his terrible cargo.

But what extraordinary thing had happened? He walked forward and knocked on the cab door of the lorry from Cornwall.

'What is it, m'dear?' said a west-country voice.

'Did a Range Rover and trailer go past you on the hard shoulder?'

'No.' The driver opened the door and dropped down to the ground. 'He'd be a fool if he tried. I reckon there's a mess ahead.'

So what happened to that tight, confident little family and their dog? Arthur Rowntree's mind was in turmoil. But he forced himself into listening to the Cornishman.

'How big a mess?' he said.

As if in answer came the wails of police cars and ambulances. Without warning, the fog started to clear. The chaos and carnage of wrecked cars and lorries ahead was plain to see.

''Strewth!' said the Cornishman.

They were on their way at last. Amy was happy now they had climbed into Daddy's lovely big green car they had bought from the funny man Dan, seen Goldie safe in his place at the back with the parcel shelf taken out, and knew her duty was to keep looking behind to make sure he kept there and the tent stayed hitched up.

Mum whispered to Dad. 'She says she had bad dreams about today.'

'Excitement,' said Dad. 'All kids get it.'

He switched on the radio. A news bulletin. A bad pile-up in the fog on the M4. Three killed, fifteen injured. Long delays until it was cleared. Caused by stupid, suicidal driving.

'Amy should have some more bad dreams,' said Dad. 'If we'd left when I wanted, we could have been in that.'

Arthur Rowntree and his west-country companion stared at the scene. Ambulances drove off, police in their dozens tried to sort things out, breakdown lorries arrived.

'It'll be a fair while before we're off,' said the Cornishman.

'I don't get it,' said Arthur Rowntree. 'There was *definitely* a D registration green Range Rover pulling a trailer tent in front of me. Golden retriever in the back. I *can't* be wrong.'

'There's no green Range Rover in that lot,' said the Cornishman, peering ahead.

'Without it, I'd have been in the back of you,' said Arthur. 'And then what?'

'Forget it,' said the Cornishman. 'It never happened.'

The fog was nearly gone: the sun gained strength. Arthur went back to his cab and brought out sandwiches and a thermos of coffee. Then he leaned up against the side of the Trelawney Transport lorry, sharing them with the Cornishman and talking companionably.

'Where are you off to, then?' said the Cornishman.

'Only Swindon. And you?'

'Nearly all the way. Not far short of Penzance. I won't get there till evening now. If this wreck makes it.'

For the first time, Arthur looked at his lorry. It was old—C registration. He knew that when it started thick black diesel fumes would choke the air.

'I keep telling Trelawney to get new lorries. "Where's the money coming from?" he says. "That doesn't mean you don't have to service them properly," I tell him. I hope I never have to stop quick going down a hill. I *know* these brakes are dodgy. One day they're going to fail on me completely. There's a bend coming down the hill to the industrial estate I'm bound for. I tremble every time I go round it. If I had to stop quick—well, I'd be over the edge, I reckon. And I'd take anything in my way with me.'

'Why drive for him, then?' said Arthur Rowntree.

'Who else is there to work for?'

Arthur Rowntree didn't answer, but watched the work going on ahead. 'They're about clear,' he said. 'We'll be on our way soon.' But his mind was still troubled. *Where* was that green Range Rover? He saw it again in his mind, every detail sharp. And then it was replaced by another vision in his mind. His friend the Cornishman, at the wheel and going round the bend on the hill leading to his destination. The two images were not to leave him all day.

The motorway ahead was clear. The sun shone and the day's heat built up. Policemen waved on the drivers who had stopped safely behind the pile-up. The Cornishman and Arthur Rowntree prepared to get back in their cabs.

'Goodbye, m'dear,' said the Cornishman.

'Safe journey,' said Arthur Rowntree. Suddenly, he felt an almost overpowering urge. He *had* to say it. 'Don't go any further. Get that death-trap off the road.'

He struggled with himself. *I should. It's my duty.* But then . . . *It's his livelihood. What right have I? It's none of my business.*

Soon they were on their way. All day, Arthur could not get rid of the two visions: the green Range Rover and the lorry which couldn't stop going down the hill. They danced before his mind's eye, merging, parting, merging again.

And behind them both were the deep brown eyes of the dog, looking at him reproachfully—as if, in some way he could not fathom, he had let the creature down.

They took their time. They stopped twice at motorway services and picnicked in Devon.

Three miles from the camping site, they overtook an old lorry: TRELAWNEY'S TRANSPORT SERVING CORNWALL. Dad was pleased: he'd been trying to pass for miles.

Mum turned to the children. 'Soon we'll go down the hill to the sea. When we're round the bend half-way down, we'll see the camping site below us.'

'Don't look at the industrial estate the other side,' said Dad.

The Cornishman watched the Range Rover and trailer pass him. A memory stirred—yes, that's like what his friend driving the tanker had been talking about, even down to the notices in the rear window and the dog, looking at him with brown eyes which caught his own and made him feel unaccountably sad. Well, if it *was* the same people, they'd had a very narrow escape this morning. Funny. Arthur had talked about them like seeing a vision. And even now, in the evening sunshine, the outline of the Range Rover seemed picked out in extraordinary hardness and its dark green paintwork shone with a lustre somehow beyond the normal. Was *he* seeing a vision? Would they disappear as soon as he looked for them again?

Of course not. They'd just come here to enjoy lovely old Cornwall. He silently wished them a good holiday as they dwindled away ahead of him. They deserved it.

Yet there was something cold and dead now in the pit of his stomach. He wanted rid of it. He was nearly at journey's end and was thankful. He longed to see the depot, his load got rid of, the front door of his house and his wife waiting.

'Here's the top of the hill,' said Mum.

The sea, blue in evening sunshine, stretched far away.

'Soon round the bend,' said Dad. 'Then we'll see the camp site.'

Before they reached the bend there was a notice warning drivers of roadworks and temporary traffic lights. Just round the bend was another notice:

WHEN RED LIGHT SHOWS, STOP HERE.

The lights had only been set up that day, as the road repairs started. They turned red just as Dad reached them, so he had to stop.

Amy suddenly started crying.

'What's the matter, love?' said Mum in alarm.

'I can see my dream again,' Amy wailed.

Goldie put his paw across the back of the seat and touched her. He whimpered slightly, as if to say, 'I tried.'

At that moment, the Cornishman in his old lorry with bad brakes reached the top of the hill.

If they're ever going to fail, he thought, *it's here and now.*

His foot, resting over the brake pedal, began to push.

Woman of the Snow

LAFCADIO HEARN

In a village of Musashi Province, there lived two wood-cutters: Mosaku and Minokichi. At the time of which I am speaking, Mosaku was an old man; and Minokichi, his apprentice, was a lad of eighteen years. Every day they went together to a forest situated about five miles from their village. On the way to that forest there is a wide river to cross; and there is a ferryboat. Several times a bridge was built where the ferry is; but the bridge was each time carried away by a flood. No common bridge can resist the current there when the river rises.

Mosaku and Minokichi were on their way home, one very cold evening, when a great snowstorm overtook them. They reached the ferry; and they found that the boatman had gone away, leaving his boat on the other side of the river. It was no day for swimming; and the woodcutters took shelter in the ferryman's hut—thinking themselves lucky to find any shelter at all. There was no brazier in the hut, nor any place in which to make a fire: there was only enough room for two sleeping mats, with a single door, but no window. Mosaku and Minokichi fastened the door, and lay down to rest, with their straw raincoats over them. At first they did not feel very cold; and they thought that the storm would soon be over.

The old man almost immediately fell asleep; but the boy, Minokichi, lay awake a long time, listening to the awful wind, and the continual slashing of the snow against the door. The river was roaring; and the hut swayed and creaked like a junk at sea. It was a terrible storm; and the air was every moment becoming colder; and Minokichi shivered under his raincoat. But at last, in spite of the cold, he too fell asleep.

He was awakened by a showering of snow in his face. The door of the hut had been forced open; and, by the snow-light, he saw a woman in the room—a woman all in white. She was bending above Mosaku, and blowing her breath upon him— and her breath was like a bright white smoke. Almost in the same moment she turned to Minokichi, and stooped over him. He tried to cry out, but found that he could not utter any sound. The white woman bent down over him, lower and lower, until her face almost touched him; and he saw that she was very beautiful—though her eyes made him afraid.

For a little time she continued to look at him; then she smiled, and she whispered: 'I intended to treat you like the other man. But I cannot help feeling some pity for you, because you are so young . . . You are a pretty boy, Minokichi; and I will not hurt you now. But, if you ever tell anybody—even your own mother—about what you have seen this night, I shall know it; and then I will kill you . . . Remember what I say!'

With these words, she turned from him and passed through the doorway. Then he found himself able to move; and he sprang up, and looked out. But the woman was nowhere to be seen; and the snow was driving furiously into the hut. Minokichi closed the door, and secured it by fixing several billets of wood against it. He wondered if the wind had blown it open; he thought that he might have only been dreaming, and might have mistaken the gleam of the snow-light in the doorway for the figure of a white woman: but he could not be sure. He called to Mosaku, and was

frightened because the old man did not answer. He put out his
hand in the dark, and touched Mosaku's face, and found that it
was ice! Mosaku was stark and dead . . .

By dawn the storm was over; and when the ferryman returned
to his station, a little after sunrise, he found Minokichi lying
senseless beside the frozen body of Mosaku. Minokichi was

promptly cared for, and soon came to himself; but he remained a long time ill from the effects of the cold of that terrible night. He had been greatly frightened also by the old man's death; but he said nothing about the vision of the woman in white. As soon as he got well again, he returned to his calling—going alone every morning to the forest, and coming back at nightfall with his bundles of wood, which his mother helped him to sell.

One evening, in the winter of the following year, as he was on his way home, he overtook a girl who happened to be travelling by the same road. She was a tall, slim girl, very good-looking; and she answered Minokichi's greeting in a voice as pleasant to the ear as the voice of a song-bird. Then he walked beside her; and they began to talk.

The girl said that her name was O-Yuki; that she had lately lost both of her parents; and that she was going to Yedo, where she happened to have some poor relations, who might help her to find a situation as servant. Minokichi soon felt charmed by this strange girl; and the more that he looked at her, the handsomer she appeared to be. He asked her whether she was yet betrothed; and she answered, laughingly, that she was free. Then, in her turn, she asked Minokichi whether he was married, or pledged to marry; and he told her that, although he had only a widowed mother to support, the question of an 'honourable daughter-in-law' had not yet been considered, as he was very young . . .

After these confidences, they walked on for a long while without speaking; but, as the proverb declares: 'When the wish is there, the eyes can say as much as the mouth.' By the time they reached the village, they had become very much pleased with each other; and then Minokichi asked O-Yuki to rest awhile at his house. After some shy hesitation, she went there with him; and his mother made her welcome, and prepared a warm meal for her. O-Yuki behaved so nicely that Minokichi's mother took a sudden fancy to her, and persuaded her to delay her journey to Yedo. And the natural end of the matter was that Yuki never went to Yedo at all. She remained in the house, as an 'honourable daughter-in-law'.

O-Yuki proved a very good daughter-in-law. When Minokichi's

mother came to die—some five years later—her last words were words of affection and praise for the wife of her son. And O-Yuki bore Minokichi ten children, boys and girls—handsome children all of them, and very fair of skin.

The country-folk thought O-Yuki a wonderful person, by nature different from themselves. Most of the peasant-women age early; but O-Yuki, even after having become the mother of ten children, looked as young and fresh as on the day when she had first come to the village.

One night, after the children had gone to sleep, O-Yuki was sewing by the light of a paper lamp; and Minokichi, watching her, said:

'To see you sewing there, with the light on your face, makes me think of a strange thing that happened when I was a lad of eighteen. I then saw somebody as beautiful and white as you are now—indeed, she was very like you.'

Without lifting her eyes from her work, O-Yuki responded:

'Tell me about her . . . Where did you see her?'

Then Minokichi told her about the terrible night in the ferryman's hut—and about the White Woman that had stooped above him, smiling and whispering—and about the silent death of old Mosaku. And he said:

'Asleep or awake, that was the only time that I saw a being as beautiful as you. Of course, she was not a human being; and I was afraid of her—very much afraid—but she was so white! . . . Indeed, I have never been sure whether it was a dream that I saw, or the Woman of the Snow.'

O-Yuki flung down her sewing, and arose, and bowed above Minokichi where he sat, and shrieked into his face:

'It was I—I—I! Yuki it was! And I told you then that I would kill you if you ever said one word about it! . . . But for those children asleep there, I would kill you this moment! And now you had better take very, very good care of them; for if ever they have a reason to complain of you, I will treat you as you deserve!'

Even as she screamed, her voice came thin, like a crying of wind; then she melted into a bright white mist that spired to the roof-beams, and shuddered away through the smoke-hole . . . Never again was she seen.

Bridgey

BRIAN JACQUES

'S ure and aren't ducks the greatest things in all the world!'
Bridgey spoke her thoughts aloud to the white mists as
they curled in wraithlike tendrils across the surface of the
morning lake. The ducks ignored her completely, quacking and
yammering the day's business among themselves as they
waddled and trundled fussily into the water led by Rafferty, the
leader of the drakes.

Bridgey wiggled the toes of her bare feet in the mud at the
water's edge as she talked to them. The ducks were used to the
sound of the little girl's voice. 'Now don't stray too close by
those bushes on the other side. Who knows, some divvil of a fox
or ferret might devour you, feathers and all.'

Rafferty began paddling over to the very spot Bridgey had
warned them about. She stamped her foot, causing mud to
splatter the frayed hem of her skirt, and waving a willow twig

at the drake, she called out, 'Mister Rafferty, are you deaf or just disobedient? What've I told you? Get out of there this very instant!'

Rafferty did a stately turn, cruising out into the centre of the lake, with an ill-assorted two score followers in his wake. Bridgey was still shaking the stick in reprimand.

'And stay away from there, d'ye hear me, or I'll tickle your tail with this stick, so I will. Wipe that silly smile off your beak, Mister Rafferty, and that goes for the rest of you. Stay this side, where I can see you well. The lake's safe, sure there's only the ould Grimblett down there—he watches over little maids and disobedient ducks good enough, 'tis his job.'

'Bridgey!'

She flinched momentarily at the sound of her uncle's voice.

'I'm over here by the lake, Uncle Sully.'

Sully McConville trod gingerly through the mud to his small niece.

'Have y'cleaned the duckpens out, girl?'

'I have so, while you were still abed.'

'Less of your lip. How many eggs today?'

'Seven and twenty, uncle.'

Bridgey smelled the raw whiskey on her uncle's breath as he brought his unshaven face close to her. McConville's bleary red-veined eyes shifted slyly as he grabbed the willow twig from Bridgey's hand.

'Are y'telling me the truth now?'

'I am so, Uncle Sully.'

He twitched the stick close to her nose.

'If you're lyin' I'll skelp the skin off your bones, girl. I think you're going soft in the head, talking to yourself out here. What's all this about a Grimblett?'

Bridgey remained silent in the face of her uncle's sour temper. Sully growled at the mud which had seeped in through his leaky boot soles.

'Go on up to the house now. Put the kettle on for tea and boil me two eggs in it, no, make that three. I'll be taking the other two dozen in to sell at Ballymain market. Cut me three slices of white bread and put the honey jar on the table. Move yourself now!'

He snapped the twig and hurled it out into the lake, causing the ducks to quack and swim off in a half flutter. Digging a broken yellowed clay pipe out of his vest pocket Sully sucked on it. He spat noisily into the lake, calling after the girl, 'And you know what you'll get if I catch you eatin' eggs, honey or white bread, me lady.'

Bridgey called back cheerfully, 'Aye, so I do. You'll skelp the skin off me bones!'

She busied herself around the ill-equipped kitchen of the crumbling cottage, murmuring to herself happily. 'Oho, Sully McConville, don't you think yourself the big bold man now. But you'll find that you can't throw broken sticks or spit into the Grimblett's lake without the creature himself knowing it. Sure, wasn't I a witness to the whole thing meself, to say nothing of Mister Rafferty and his ducks. Small wonder they were all smilin' to themselves. Finer men than yourself haven't got away with less.'

The kettle was bubbling merrily as Bridgey spooned three duck eggs into the water. Facing the open window, she laid the well scrubbed wooden table with white bread and a brownstone crock jar of honey for her greedy uncle. There was buttermilk and two of last night's cold boiled potatoes, still in their skins, for Bridgey's breakfast. She watched Sully walk up from the lake, shaking mud from his boots and muttering darkly to himself about the injustices of life. The mist had begun to disperse under a yellow late spring sun, and Bridgey could make out the Grimblett. It was lying just beneath the clear surface of the lake, all green and misty, spreading wavery tentacles far and wide across its realm.

'You look fit and well today, Grimblett, though I can tell you're angry with me Uncle Sully, and sure, why wouldn't you be? The way he sucks that dirty pipe and spits on you every day. I'll have to go now; he's coming for his breakfast. I'll talk to you later.'

Sully McConville sat across the table from his niece, watching her as he sucked tea noisily from a chipped mug. Bridgey kept her eyes down, munching industriously on the potatoes and washing them down with sips of buttermilk. Sully wiped his mouth on the back of his sleeve.

'Eat up now, girl, and thank the Lord who left me to provide for you after your ma and da passed on. Leave a clean plate now, and thank God for his goodness and bounty.'

He cracked an egg and spooned it hastily into his mouth, yellow runny yolk dribbling through the coarse whiskers on to his chin. Tearing a crust from the bread he dipped it in the honey and sucked noisily on it. Bridgey could not help the disgust which showed on her face. Sully wagged the crust at her across the table.

'Straighten your gob, girl, or I'll skelp the skin off your bones. Duck eggs are too rich for children and the honey would only bring you out in a rash of pimples. I need it for me chest.' Here he coughed to illustrate the point. 'Taters and buttermilk are what I was brought up on. They never harmed me, so you eat up now.'

'I will, uncle.'

'And don't waste any. There's goodness in potato skins.'

'I'm not wasting any at all, uncle.'

'Well make sure you don't.'

Bridgey would rather have died than eat a duck egg. The ducks were her friends and she had seen the ducklings that came from the eggs, little, downy, smiling creatures, with tiny comical wings. But white bread and honey, that was a different matter altogether. She had dipped soft white bread into the honey when her uncle was absent—it tasted like heaven on earth. Then one day Sully had caught her; he had beaten her soundly with a blackthorn stick he kept behind the door. Bridgey had never stolen bread and honey again, though she often dreamed of the bread, with its fresh smell and crispy crust, together with the sweet, heavy, mysterious stickiness of deep amber honey, with chewy fragments of combwax which clung to the teeth. Sully's voice broke in on her imaginings.

'Right, I'm off now to the Ballymain market. Mind you boil those taters the way I like them, so they're floury when they split. See to the ducks, put fresh straw in their pens, and tidy up around here. Sweep the floor, wash the dishes and scrub the table well. I'll be back at nightfall, and you know what'll happen to you if there's anything amiss, Bridgey.'

'You'll skelp the skin off me bones, uncle.'

'Aye, so I will.'

Sully licked honey from his whiskers, belched, lighted his pipe and set his hat on squarely. Then he left for Ballymain market.

The afternoon was peaceful; under the warm sun the lake lay smooth and placid. Even the ducks had stopped paddling; they floated about silently, napping in the noontide. Mister Rafferty stood on the bank, gently squelching the mud under his webbed feet. Though he was facing away from the house his bright little eye oscillated backwards, as he watched Bridgey come to the water's edge, her bare feet disturbing the thin crust that the sun had baked upon the mud. Rafferty gave a short quack of welcome, declining to comment further on the loaf and honey crock which the little girl placed upon a stone. She sat down next to them. The drake wandered over, his slim graceful neck nodding slightly as he waddled. Bridgey passed her hand gently over his sleek head.

'Good afternoon to you, sir. Have you had enough of the swimming?'

Mister Rafferty nodded and settled down by her.

'Ah well, your family look all nice and peaceful there. See Matilda with her head beneath her wing, fast asleep, Lord love her.'

Drake and girl sat watching the water. Bridgey half closed her eyes and began intoning in a soft singsong voice.

'Grimblett, Grimblett, are you there?'

The lake stayed calm and unruffled.

'I know for sure you're out there, Grimblett. Will y'not bid me a good afternoon?'

Out upon the middle of the waters a single large bubble plopped and gurgled, causing ripples to widen across the surface. Bridgey and Mister Rafferty nodded knowingly.

'Ah, you're still angered over Sully spittin' and throwing sticks at you this morning.'

Once more the lake bubbled and gurgled. This time a frond of the heavy green weed that lay beneath the surface rose momentarily clear of the waters; then it slid back under. Bridgey sighed. 'Well, I'm sorry for you, but there's little Rafferty or I can do.'

A huge bubble, like an upturned bathtub, gurgled its way into the noon air; more ripples began, stretching in circles until small waves lapped over Bridgey's toes. She stood up.

'I'll tell you what I'll do, Grimblett. I'll pour a bit of this honey to you, some bread and all. That should make you feel better, eh?'

This time the lake lay still.

Bridgey broke the bread and scattered it on the water. Immediately the ducks came awake and swam over to gobble it up, though Mister Rafferty remained faithfully at her side. Bridgey picked up the honey crock.

'Oh come on now, Grimblett, don't be sulking on such a fine afternoon. See, you were too late to get the bread, now Mister Rafferty's family've eaten it. Here, try some honey. You'll like it, the taste is like flowers and meadows in summer. Come on now.'

Bridgey tilted the crock, shaking it vigorously to make the honey flow. Rafferty watched her intently. The honey did not seem too keen on leaving its container, though a very small amount oozed out on to Bridgey's fingers. She licked the stickiness and rinsed her hands in the lake, cajoling her friend the Grimblett.

'Ah c'mon now, don't be shy. You'll enjoy it.'

Upending the crock, she shook it hard. The smooth glazed earthenware jar shot from between her wet hands and rolled away underwater down the steep lake bed before Bridgey could do anything about it. She slumped on the stone, holding her hands across her eyes, trying not to believe what she had just done.

'Heaven preserve me, Uncle Sully will skelp the skin off me bones with his blackthorn stick. I know he will, he'll have me very life! Grimblett, is there nothing you can do to save a little maid. Roll the crock back to me. Oh please!'

The water bubbled apologetically and lay calm. Mister Rafferty placed his bill sympathetically in Bridgey's lap as his family paddled close in and floated there, watching her. Slow minutes of the sunny noontide ebbed inexorably away. Bridgey's tears flowed along with them.

Nothing could hold back time and the return of Sully McConville from Ballymain market. Bridgey had cried herself to sleep by the lake; she wakened with the slight chill of advancing eventide to a reddening sky in which the sun sank gloriously, like a peach dipped into port wine. Hurrying to the house Bridgey rushed about like a dervish, setting the pot of potatoes on its tripod over the fire and tossing in a dash of salt.

As if to redeem her quivering flesh from the crime she had committed, the little girl set about her chores with furious energy, piling turf on the fire, scrubbing the table, sweeping the hard packed earth floor with a besom until dust flew widespread, wiping that same dust from shelf, table, chair and windows with a cheesecloth. She put just the right amount of leaves into the battered teapot and trimmed the lamp wick to even the flame as darkness fell. Inside, the cottage was as fresh as new paint. Bridgey stood at the open door, her heart beating fitfully against the leaden weight within her chest as she watched her Uncle Sully staggering up the path through the darkness.

It was evident that he had been drinking by the way he weaved to and fro. Under his arm Sully carried a bottle and a piece of smoke-cured bacon from Ballymain market, to supplement his supper of boiled potatoes. He brushed past Bridgey and sat heavily in his chair, slamming down the bacon upon the table.

'Bridgey, slice some of this up an' fry it for me, a man needs some meat now and again. It's no good for children, mind, too fat an' salty. Well, don't stand there gawpin' with cow's eyes, move yourself, girl, or it'll be mornin' soon.'

With trembling hands she cut the bacon into rough slices, setting it on the frying pan to sizzle as she drained off the water from the potatoes . . . fearful that any moment her uncle might call for bread and honey. Sully, however, was not looking to satisfy his sweet tooth, not while there was whiskey to be had. Weary and footsore after the long trek home from Ballymain, he kicked off his boots and pulled the chair up to the fire. Lighting his clay pipe with a spill, he started drinking straight from the bottle. Bridgey worked with quick, nervous energy, laying out his plate of food at the table and pouring a mug of tea for him. She gave a fearful start at the sound of Sully's voice.

'Is that the ducks I can hear still out on the lake, girl?'

'Ducks? Oh, I must have forgotten, I'll get them into the pen right away. Come and have your supper, Uncle Sully. It's on the table, all nice and hot.'

He swigged at the bottle. His pipe lay forgotten on the hearth.

'I'll Uncle Sully you, idle little faggot. Never mind the supper, you get those ducks in or I'll skelp the skin off your bones!'

Bridgey fled the cottage, hurrying through the night to the water's edge. Mister Rafferty stood on the bank. Cocking his head on one side he quacked wearily. Bridgey could make out the shapes of other ducks, asleep on the far bank.

'Oh Mister Rafferty, there you are. I'm sorry I forgot to take you and your family to the pens. You've not been fed either. 'Tis all me own fault, I'm a terrible girl.'

The drake stretched himself. Spreading his wings he quacked aloud his various complaints. Bridgey cast an uneasy glance at the cottage. 'Hush now, or you'll have me uncle out here with his great stick. Listen, we'll never get those others off the far bank until morning. You bide here and hold your noise, I've got to go back to the house. I promise you'll come to no harm, the Grimblett will watch over you and your family, I know he will.'

Mister Rafferty settled his neck down on his crop feathers as Bridgey ran off into the darkness. Behind him the surface of the lake threw up a few bubbles before subsiding into the calm of a late spring night.

Bridgey breathed a small sob of relief; Uncle Sully had fallen asleep in his chair by the fire. Carefully she removed the quarter full whiskey bottle from between his limp fingers and set it on the table, alongside the now cold bacon and potatoes. It was not unusual for him to sleep all night in front of the fire, fully dressed, after he had been drinking. Safe for the night at least, Bridgey backed up the fire with damp slow-burning turf. Taking some potatoes in a clean piece of cloth she went back to the lake with an old shawl wrapped about her shoulders. Sully McConville snored gently, his mouth half open, chin on chest and hands lying loosely upon his stomach as it heaved up and down in the flickering shadows of the warm room.

Out by the lake Bridgey perched on a stone, sharing her meal of cold cooked potato with Mister Rafferty. A thin moon sliver hung over the lake like a slice of lemon rind, turning the water to a light golden shimmer, backed by the silhouette of the trees which massed on the far lakeshore. Bridgey murmured softly to her friend, 'There's a fear in me for what the morn will bring. I wish it could stay peaceful night forever, so I do.'

Beside her the drake blinked his bright little eyes and smiled that secret smile that only ducks and drakes know the meaning of.

Sully groaned aloud as morning sunlight cascaded through the window panes to set his brain afire. Flaming orange motes danced a jig before his half opened eyes; sour whiskey taste clogged his furred tongue as his temples thrummed with the father of all headaches. In a petulant croak he called out, 'Bridgey, bring the honey, girl!'

There was no answer. Sully heaved himself painfully out of his chair. The embers of the fire were hidden beneath thick grey ash. With ill-tempered bile rising within him he glared at the cold teapot beside the cold bacon and potatoes on the table. Tripping over his boots he cursed and kicked at them.

'Bridgey, bring me the honey an' a spoon, or I'll skelp the skin off your bones. Bridgey, where are y'girl?'

Stumbling and muttering he searched shelf and cupboard for the crock, longing for the soothing sweetness of honey to drive away the whiskey bitterness from his mouth. The quacking of unfed ducks down at the lake diverted his attention. He fumbled with the latch and swung the door ajar, wincing at the stream of sunlight which shafted in like a volley of golden arrows.

There she was, the idle little faggot, curled up on a stone with a shawl around her and that cheeky ould drake. This time he would teach her a lesson that she'd remember to her dying day!

Snatching the blackthorn stick from behind the door he roared like a wounded lion.

'Bridgeeeeeeee!'

Like a shot the little girl sprang up. Mister Rafferty, quacking and ruffled, slid from her knees awkwardly. Bridgey's face went white with fright at the sight of her uncle brandishing the blackthorn stick as he strode barefoot towards her.

'Er, er, top of the mornin' to you, sir, I was about to feed the ducks.'

A large vein stood out on Sully's temple, pulsing like a

nightingale's throat. His voice was thick and harsh.

'Feed the ducks, is it? What about me, don't I get fed? The place is like a midden—cold food, no fire, no tea or honey, and you out here sleepin' your shiftless life away!'

Sully had begun moving this way and that, cutting off any possible retreat. Bridgey had the lake at her back. There was no way she might avoid a skelping.

'Uncle, I'm sorry, it wasn't my fault. Me hands were wet an' the honey crock slipped off into the water. I'll never do it again.'

Sully smiled wickedly, raising the heavy stick.

'So, you'll not do it again, eh, girl. You'll be lucky if you have legs to stand on after I'm done with you, me lazy scut!'

He swung the stick in a vicious arc. Bridgey dodged to one side. Sully slipped and fell heavily in the mud; he came up shouting and covered in brown slime.

'Cummere, I'll skelp the skin off your bo—'

And then Mister Rafferty was upon him, quacking and flapping. As if on a given signal the ducks came out with a rush from the water and piled in on Sully. Bridgey could hardly make out her uncle—he was enveloped in hissing, quacking, feather-beating, web-clawing birds. Sully lost the blackthorn stick in the mud, frantically he beat about, his arms milling wide, slipping, falling, skidding in the slutchy mud as he ranted and roared.

'I'll kill yeh, d'you hear me! I'll wring your blasted necks!'

Out in the middle of the lake bubbles began bursting on the surface. Bridgey cried aloud in terror.

'Save us, Grimblett! Oh do something, please!'

Sully thrust the birds from him with a mighty effort and stepped backwards to gain a breathing space.

But he stepped back into the lake!

He slid in the sloping shallows and overbalanced. Blowing water from his nostrils and wiping his face upon a wet sleeve he stood there, his clawing hands shaking at Bridgey.

'I'll throttle the life from yeh, you and those ducks!'

The lake behind Sully McConville began bubbling madly, as if the waters were boiling. He tried pulling himself forward but slid further backwards. Something was wrapped around his feet; he felt the water lapping about his chest. A look of fear crossed his ugly features.

'Bridgey, help me, girl. Help me!'

Now the thick, trailing green fronds appeared. They draped about his arms and neck, caressing him with coldness they had fetched up from the depths. Sully tried feebly to fight against them, but they piled upon him like the tentacles of some unknown emerald monster. Colossal bubbles created waves upon the lake that filled his mouth and flooded his ears.

'Save me, girl, Bridgeeeeeeee!'

She watched, fascinated, as a waving sloppy frond wrapped itself around her uncle's mouth and nostrils, stifling his cries forever. Back, back he was dragged until he vanished beneath the surface. The waters gave one final bulking swirl; a single bubble burst up from the depths into the sunlight. Then calm reigned over the scene. To any passing traveller it would have made a charming rustic picture: the little ragged girl standing in the sunshine with her ducks on the banks of a quiet lake.

Sully McConville's boots burned merrily on the turf fire. Bridgey sat in his chair, Mister Rafferty at her feet like a faithful pet dog. Ducks perched on the shelf, windowsill and table, some of them eating the remains of the cold potatoes from the supper plate. Bridgey stirred the drake gently with her bare foot.

'Mister Rafferty, d'you think you could tell your family to lay lots of eggs? Then in a day or two perhaps you and me will go to Ballymain market and get more honey, white bread too. You'd like that, wouldn't you? Sure it's grand stuff the honey is.'

She rose and went to lean on the windowsill, gazing out at the lake. 'And yourself, Grimblett, we'll bring honey back for you and all. Sure, it'll help you get rid of the nasty taste, so it will.'

The Ash-Tree

M. R. JAMES

Everyone who has travelled over Eastern England knows the smaller country-houses with which it is studded— the rather dank little buildings, usually in the Italian style, surrounded with parks of some eighty to a hundred acres. For me they have always had a very strong attraction, with the grey paling of split oak, the noble trees, the meres with their reed-beds, and the line of distant woods. Then, I like the pillared portico—perhaps stuck on to a red-brick Queen Anne house which has been faced with stucco to bring it into line with the 'Grecian' taste of the end of the eighteenth century; the hall inside, going up to the roof, which hall ought always to be provided with a gallery and a small organ. I like the library, too, where you may find anything from a Psalter of the thirteenth century to a Shakespeare quarto. I like the pictures, of course; and perhaps most of all I like fancying what life in such a house was when it was first built, and in the piping times of landlords' prosperity, and not least now, when, if money is not so plentiful, taste is more varied and life quite as interesting. I wish to have one of these houses, and enough money to keep it together and entertain my friends in it modestly.

But this is a digression. I have to tell you of a curious series of events which happened in such a house as I have tried to describe. It is Castringham Hall in Suffolk. I think a good deal has been done to the building since the period of my story, but the essential features I have sketched are still there—Italian portico, square block of white house, older inside than out, park with fringe of woods, and mere. The one feature that marked out the house from a score of others is gone. As you looked at it from the park, you saw on the right a great old ash-tree growing within half a dozen yards of the wall, and almost or quite touching the building with its branches. I suppose it had stood there ever since Castringham ceased to be a fortified place, and since the moat was filled in and the Elizabethan dwelling-house built. At any rate, it had well-nigh attained its full dimensions in the year 1690.

In that year the district in which the Hall is situated was the scene of a number of witch-trials. It will be long, I think, before we arrive at a just estimate of the amount of solid reason—if there was any—which lay at the root of the universal fear of witches in old times. Whether the persons accused of this offence really did imagine that they were possessed of unusual power of any kind; or whether they had the will at least, if not the power, of doing mischief to their neighbours; or whether all the confessions, of which there are so many, were extorted by the cruelty of the witch-finders—these are questions which are not, I fancy, yet solved. And the present narrative gives me pause. I cannot altogether sweep it away as mere invention. The reader must judge for himself.

Castringham contributed a victim to the *auto-da-fé*. Mrs Mothersole was her name, and she differed from the ordinary run of village witches only in being rather better off and in a more influential position. Efforts were made to save her by several reputable farmers of the parish. They did their best to testify to her character, and showed considerable anxiety as to the verdict of the jury.

But what seems to have been fatal to the woman was the evidence of the then proprietor of Castringham Hall—Sir Matthew Fell. He deposed to having watched her on three different occasions from his window, at the full of the moon, gathering sprigs 'from the ash-tree near my house'. She had climbed into the branches, clad only in her shift, and was cutting off small twigs with a peculiarly curved knife, and as she did so she seemed to be talking to herself. On each occasion Sir Matthew had done his best to capture the woman, but she had always taken alarm at some accidental noise he had made, and all he could see when he got down to the garden was a hare running across the path in the direction of the village.

On the third night he had been at the pains to follow at his best speed, and had gone straight to Mrs Mothersole's house; but he had had to wait a quarter of an hour battering at her door, and then she had come out very cross, and apparently very sleepy, as if just out of bed; and he had no good explanation to offer of his visit.

Mainly on this evidence, though there was much more of a less striking and unusual kind from other parishioners, Mrs Mothersole was found guilty and condemned to die. She was hanged a week after the trial, with five or six more unhappy creatures, at Bury St Edmunds.

Sir Matthew Fell, then Deputy-Sheriff, was present at the execution. It was a damp, drizzly March morning when the cart made its way up the rough grass hill outside Northgate, where the gallows stood. The other victims were apathetic or broken down with misery; but Mrs Mothersole was, as in life so in death, of a very different temper. Her 'poysonous Rage', as a reporter of the time puts it, 'did so work upon the Bystanders— yea, even upon the Hangman—that it was constantly affirmed of all that saw her that she presented the living Aspect of a mad Divell. Yet she offer'd no Resistance to the Officers of the Law; onely she looked upon those that laid Hands upon her with so direfull and venomous an Aspect that—as one of them after-wards assured me—the meer Thought of it preyed inwardly upon his Mind for six Months after.'

However, all that she is reported to have said were the seemingly meaningless words: 'There will be guests at the Hall.' Which she repeated more than once in an undertone.

Sir Matthew Fell was not unimpressed by the bearing of the woman. He had some talk upon the matter with the vicar of his parish, with whom he travelled home after the assize business was over. His evidence at the trial had not been very willingly given; he was not specially infected with the witch-finding mania, but he declared, then and afterwards, that he could not give any other account of the matter than that he had given, and that he could not possibly have been mistaken as to what he saw. The whole transaction had been repugnant to him, for he was a man who liked to be on pleasant terms with those about him; but he saw a duty to be done in this business, and he had done it. That seems to have been the gist of his sentiments, and the vicar applauded it, as any reasonable man must have done.

A few weeks after, when the moon of May was at the full, vicar and squire met again in the park, and walked to the Hall together. Lady Fell was with her mother, who was dangerously ill, and Sir Matthew was alone at home; so the vicar, Mr Crome, was easily persuaded to take a late supper at the Hall.

Sir Matthew was not very good company this evening. The talk ran chiefly on family and parish matters, and, as luck would have it, Sir Matthew made a memorandum in writing of certain wishes or intentions of his regarding his estates, which after- wards proved exceedingly useful.

When Mr Crome thought of starting for home, about half past nine o'clock, Sir Matthew and he took a preliminary turn on the gravelled walk at the back of the house. The only incident that struck Mr Crome was this: they were in sight of the ash-tree which I described as growing near the windows of the building, when Sir Matthew stopped and said:

'What is that that runs up and down the stem of the ash? It is never a squirrel? They will all be in their nests by now.'

The vicar looked and saw the moving creature, but he could make nothing of its colour in the moonlight. The sharp outline, however, seen for an instant, was imprinted on his brain, and he could have sworn, he said, though it sounded foolish, that, squirrel or not, it had more than four legs.

Still, not much was to be made of the momentary vision, and the two men parted. They may have met since then, but it was not for a score of years.

Next day Sir Matthew Fell was not downstairs at six in the

morning, as was his custom, nor at seven, nor yet at eight. Hereupon the servants went and knocked at his chamber door. I need not prolong the description of their anxious listenings and renewed batterings on the panels. The door was opened at last from the outside, and they found their master dead and black. So much you have guessed. That there were any marks of violence did not at the moment appear; but the window was open.

One of the men went to fetch the parson, and then by his directions rode on to give notice to the coroner. Mr Crome himself went as quick as he might to the Hall, and was shown to the room where the dead man lay. He has left some notes among his papers which show how genuine a respect and sorrow was felt for Sir Matthew, and there is also this passage, which I transcribe for the sake of the light it throws upon the course of events, and also upon the common beliefs of the time:

'There was not any the least Trace of an Entrance having been forc'd to the Chamber: but the Casement stood open, as my poor Friend would always have it in this Season. He had his Evening Drink of small Ale in a silver vessel of about a pint measure, and tonight had not drunk it out. This Drink was examined by the Physician from Bury, a Mr Hodgkins, who could not, however, as he afterwards declar'd upon his Oath, before the Coroner's quest, discover that any matter of a venomous kind was present in it. For, as was natural, in the great Swelling and Blackness of the Corpse, there was talk made among the Neighbours of Poyson.

'The Body was very much Disorder'd as it laid in the Bed, being twisted after so extream a sort as gave too probable Conjecture that my worthy Friend and Patron had expir'd in great Pain and Agony. And what is as yet unexplain'd, and to myself the Argument of some Horrid and Artfull Designe in the Perpetrators of this Barbarous Murther, was this, that the Women which were entrusted with the laying-out of the Corpse and washing it, being both sad Pearsons and very well Respected in their Mournfull Profession, came to me in a great Pain and Distress both of Mind and Body, saying, what was indeed confirmed upon the first View, that they had no sooner touch'd the Breast of the Corpse with their naked Hands than they were sensible of a more than ordinary violent Smart and

Acheing in their Palms, which, with their whole Forearms, in no long time swell'd so immoderately, the Pain still continuing, that, as afterwards proved, during many weeks they were forc'd to lay by the exercise of their Calling; and yet no mark seen on the Skin.

'Upon hearing this, I sent for the Physician, who was still in the House, and we made as carefull a Proof as we were able by the Help of a small Magnifying Lens of Crystal of the condition of the Skinn on this Part of the Body: but could not detect with the Instrument we had any Matter of Importance beyond a couple of small Punctures or Pricks, which we then concluded were the Spotts by which the Poyson might be introduced, remembering the Ring of *Pope Borgia,* with other known Specimens of the Horrid Art of the Italian Poysoners of the last age.

'So much is to be said of the Symptoms seen on the Corpse. As to what I am to add, it is meerly my own Experiment, and to be left to Posterity to judge whether there be anything of Value therein. There was on the Table by the Beddside a Bible of the small size, in which my Friend—punctuall as in Matters of less Moment, so in this more weighty one—used nightly, and upon his First Rising, to read a sett Portion. And I taking it up—not without a Tear duly paid to him wich from the Study of this poorer Adumbration was now pass'd to the contemplation of its great Originall—it came into my Thoughts, as at such moments of Helplessness we are prone to catch at any the least Glimmer that makes promise of Light, to make trial of that old and by many accounted Superstitious Practice of drawing the *Sortes;* of which a Principall Instance, in the case of his late Sacred Majesty the Blessed Martyr King *Charles* and my Lord *Falkland,* was now much talked of. I must needs admit that by my Trial not much Assistance was afforded me: yet, as the Cause and Origin of these Dreadfull Events may hereafter be search'd out, I set down the Results, in the case it may be found that they pointed the true Quarter of the Mischief to a quicker Intelligence than my own.

'I made, then, three trials, opening the Book and placing my Finger upon certain Words: which gave in the first these words, from Luke xiii. 7, *Cut it down;* in the second, Isaiah xiii. 20, *It shall never be inhabited;* and upon the third Experiment, Job xxxix. 30, *Her young ones also suck up blood.*'

This is all that need be quoted from Mr Crome's papers. Sir Matthew Fell was duly coffined and laid into the earth, and his funeral sermon, preached by Mr Crome on the following Sunday, has been printed under the title of 'The Unsearchable Way; or, England's Danger and the Malicious Dealings of Antichrist', it being the vicar's view, as well as that most commonly held in the neighbourhood, that the squire was the victim of a recrudescence of the Popish Plot.

His son, Sir Matthew the second, succeeded to the title and estates. And so ends the first act of the Castringham tragedy. It is to be mentioned, though the fact is not surprising, that the new baronet did not occupy the room in which his father had died. Nor, indeed, was it slept in by anyone but an occasional visitor during the whole of his occupation. He died in 1735, and I do not find that anything particular marked his reign, save a curiously constant mortality among his cattle and live-stock in general, which showed a tendency to increase slightly as time went on.

Those who are interested in the details will find a statistical account in a letter to the *Gentleman's Magazine* of 1772, which draws the facts from the baronet's own papers. He put an end to it at last by a very simple expedient, that of shutting up all his beasts in sheds at night, and keeping no sheep in his park. For he had noticed that nothing was ever attacked that spent the night indoors. After that the disorder confined itself to wild birds, and beasts of chase. But as we have no good account of the symptoms, and as all-night watching was quite unproductive of any clue, I do not dwell on what the Suffolk farmers called the 'Castringham sickness'.

The second Sir Matthew died in 1735, as I said, and was duly succeeded by his son, Sir Richard. It was in his time that the great family pew was built out on the north side of the parish church. So large were the squire's ideas that several of the graves on that unhallowed side of the building had to be disturbed to satisfy his requirements. Among them was that of Mrs Mothersole, the position of which was accurately known, thanks to a note on a plan of the church and yard, both made by Mr Crome.

A certain amount of interest was excited in the village when it was known that the famous witch, who was still remembered by a few, was to be exhumed. And the feeling of surprise, and indeed disquiet, was very strong when it was found that, though her coffin was fairly sound and unbroken, there was no trace whatever inside it of body, bones, or dust. Indeed, it is a curious phenomenon, for at the time of her burying no such things were dreamt of as resurrection-men, and it is difficult to conceive any rational motive for stealing a body otherwise than for the uses of the dissecting-room.

The incident revived for a time all the stories of witch-trials and of the exploits of the witches, dormant for forty years, and Sir Richard's orders that the coffin should be burnt were thought by a good many to be rather foolhardy, though they were duly carried out.

Sir Richard was a pestilent innovator, it is certain. Before his time the Hall had been a fine block of the mellowest red brick; but Sir Richard had travelled in Italy and become infected with the Italian taste, and, having more money than his predecessors, he determined to leave an Italian palace where he had found an English house. So stucco and ashlar masked the brick; some indifferent Roman marbles were planted about in the entrance-hall and gardens; a reproduction of the Sibyl's temple at Tivoli was erected on the opposite bank of the mere; and Castringham took on an entirely new, and, I must say, a less engaging, aspect. But it was much admired, and served as a model to a good many of the neighbouring gentry in after-years.

One morning (it was in 1754) Sir Richard woke after a night of discomfort. It had been windy, and his chimney had smoked persistently, and yet it was so cold that he must keep up a fire. Also something had so rattled about the window that no man could get a moment's peace. Further, there was the prospect of several guests of position arriving in the course of the day, who would expect sport of some kind, and the inroads of the distemper (which continued among his game) had been lately so serious that he was afraid for his reputation as a game-preserver. But what really touched him most nearly was the other matter of his sleepless night. He could certainly not sleep in that room again.

That was the chief subject of his meditations at breakfast, and after it he began a systematic examination of the rooms to see which would suit his notions best. It was long before he found one. This had a window with an eastern aspect and that with a northern; this door the servants would be always passing, and he did not like the bedstead in that. No, he must have a room with a western look-out, so that the sun could not wake him early, and it must be out of the way of the business of the house. The housekeeper was at the end of her resources.

'Well, Sir Richard,' she said, 'you know that there is but the one room like that in the house.'

'Which may that be?' said Sir Richard.

'And that is Sir Matthew's—the West Chamber.'

'Well, put me in there, for there I'll lie tonight,' said her master. 'Which way is it? Here, to be sure'; and he hurried off.

'Oh, Sir Richard, but no one has slept there these forty years. The air has hardly been changed since Sir Matthew died there.'

Thus she spoke, and rustled after him.

'Come, open the door, Mrs Chiddock. I'll see the chamber, at least.'

So it was opened, and, indeed, the smell was very close and earthy. Sir Richard crossed to the window, and, impatiently, as was his wont, threw the shutters back, and flung open the casement. For this end of the house was one which the alterations had barely touched, grown up as it was with the great ash-tree, and being otherwise concealed from view.

'Air it, Mrs Chiddock, all today, and move my bed-furniture in in the afternoon. Put the Bishop of Kilmore in my old room.'

'Pray, Sir Richard,' said a new voice, breaking in on this speech, 'might I have the favour of a moment's interview?'

Sir Richard turned round and saw a man in black in the doorway, who bowed.

'I must ask your indulgence for this intrusion, Sir Richard. You will, perhaps, hardly remember me. My name is William Crome, and my grandfather was vicar in your grandfather's time.'

'Well, sir,' said Sir Richard, 'the name of Crome is always a passport to Castringham. I am glad to renew a friendship of two generations' standing. In what can I serve you? for your hour of calling—and, if I do not mistake you, your bearing—shows you to be in some haste.'

'That is no more than the truth, sir. I am riding from Norwich to Bury St Edmonds with what haste I can make, and I have called in on my way to leave with you some papers which we have but just come upon in looking over what my grandfather left at his death. It is thought you may find some matters of family interest in them.'

'You are mighty obliging, Mr Crome, and, if you will be so good as to follow me to the parlour, and drink a glass of wine, we will take a first look at these same papers together. And you, Mrs Chiddock, as I said, be about airing this chamber . . . Yes, it is here my grandfather died . . . Yes, the tree, perhaps, does make the place a little dampish . . . No; I do not wish to listen to any more. Make no difficulties, I beg. You have your orders—go. Will you follow me, sir?'

They went to the study. The packet which young Mr Crome had brought—he was then just become a Fellow of Clare Hall in Cambridge, I may say, and subsequently brought out a respectable edition of Polyaenus—contained among other things the notes which the old vicar had made upon the occasion of Sir Matthew Fell's death. And for the first time Sir Richard was confronted with the enigmatical *Sortes Biblicae* which you have heard. They amused him a good deal.

'Well,' he said, 'my grandfather's Bible gave one prudent piece of advice—*Cut it down*. If that stands for the ash-tree, he may rest assured I shall not neglect it. Such a nest of catarrhs and agues was never seen.'

The parlour contained the family books, which, pending the arrival of a collection which Sir Richard had made in Italy, and the building of a proper room to receive them, were not many in number.

Sir Richard looked up from the paper to the bookcase.

'I wonder,' says he, 'whether the old prophet is there yet? I fancy I see him.'

Crossing the room, he took out a dumpy Bible, which, sure enough, bore on the flyleaf the inscription: 'To Matthew Fell, from his Loving Godmother, Anne Aldous, 2 September 1659.'

'It would be no bad plan to test him again, Mr Crome. I will wager we get a couple of names in the Chronicles. H'm! what have we here? "Thou shalt seek me in the morning, and I shall not be." Well, well! Your grandfather would have made a fine omen of that, hey? No more prophets for me! They are all in a tale. And now, Mr Crome, I am infinitely obliged to you for your packet. You will, I fear, be impatient to get on. Pray allow me—another glass.'

So with offers of hospitality, which were genuinely meant (for Sir Richard thought well of the young man's address and manner), they parted.

In the afternoon came the guests—the Bishop of Kilmore, Lady Mary Hervey, Sir William Kentfield, etc. Dinner at five, wine, cards, supper, and dispersal to bed.

Next morning Sir Richard is disinclined to take his gun with the rest. He talks with the Bishop of Kilmore. This prelate, unlike a good many of the Irish bishops of his day, had visited his see, and, indeed, resided there, for some considerable time. This morning, as the two were walking along the terrace and talking over the alterations and improvements in the house, the bishop said, pointing to the window of the West Room:

'You could never get one of my Irish flock to occupy that room, Sir Richard.'

'Why is that, my lord? It is, in fact, my own.'

'Well, our Irish peasantry will always have it that it brings the worst of luck to sleep near an ash-tree, and you have a fine growth of ash not two yards from your chamber window. Perhaps,' the bishop went on, with a smile, 'it has given you a touch of its quality already, for you do not seem, if I may say it, so much the fresher for your night's rest as your friends would like to see you.'

'That, or something else, it is true, cost me my sleep from twelve to four, my lord. But the tree is to come down tomorrow, so I shall not hear much more from it.'

'I applaud your determination. It can hardly be wholesome to have the air you breathe strained, as it were, through all that leafage.'

'Your lordship is right there, I think. But I had not my window open last night. It was rather the noise that went on— no doubt from the twigs sweeping the glass—that kept me open-eyed.'

'I think that can hardly be, Sir Richard. Here—you see it from this point. None of these nearest branches even can touch your casement unless there were a gale, and there was none of that last night. They miss the panes by a foot.'

'No, sir, true. What, then, will it be, I wonder, that scratched and rustled so—ay, and covered the dust on my sill with lines and marks?'

At last they agreed that the rats must have come up through the ivy. That was the bishop's idea, and Sir Richard jumped at it.

So the day passed quietly, and night came, and the party dispersed to their rooms, and wished Sir Richard a better night.

And now we are in his bedroom, with the light out and the squire in bed. The room is over the kitchen, and the night outside still and warm, so the window stands open.

There is very little light about the bedstead, but there is a strange movement there; it seems as if Sir Richard were moving his head rapidly to and fro with only the slightest possible sound. And now you would guess, so deceptive is the half-darkness, that he had several heads, round and brownish, which move back and forward, even as low as his chest. It is a horrible illusion. Is it nothing more? There! something drops off the bed with a soft plump, like a kitten, and is out of the window in a flash; another—four—and after that there is quiet again.

Thou shalt seek me in the morning, and I shall not be.

As with Sir Matthew, so with Sir Richard—dead and black in his bed!

A pale and silent party of guests and servants gathered under the window when the news was known. Italian poisoners, Popish emissaries, infected air—all these and more guesses were hazarded, and the Bishop of Kilmore looked at the tree, in the fork of whose lower boughs a white tom-cat was crouching, looking down the hollow which years had gnawed in the trunk. It was watching something inside the tree with great interest.

Suddenly it got up and craned over the hole. Then a bit of the edge on which it stood gave way, and it went slithering in. Everyone looked up at the noise of the fall.

It is known to most of us that a cat can cry; but few of us have heard, I hope, such a yell as came out of the trunk of the great ash. Two or three screams there were—the witnesses are not sure which—and then a slight and muffled noise of some commotion or struggling was all that came. But Lady Mary

Hervey fainted outright, and the housekeeper stopped her ears and fled till she fell on the terrace.

The Bishop of Kilmore and Sir William Kentfield stayed. Yet even they were daunted, though it was only at the cry of a cat; and Sir William swallowed once or twice before he could say:

'There is something more than we know of in that tree, my lord. I am for an instant search.'

And this was agreed upon. A ladder was brought, and one of the gardeners went up, and, looking down the hollow, could detect nothing but a few dim indications of something moving. They got a lantern, and let it down by a rope.

'We must get at the bottom of this. My life upon it, my lord, but the secret of these terrible deaths is there.'

Up went the gardener again with the lantern, and let it down the hole cautiously. They saw the yellow light upon his face as he bent over, and saw his face struck with an incredulous terror and loathing before he cried out in a dreadful voice and fell back from the ladder—where, happily, he was caught by two of the men—letting the lantern fall inside the tree.

He was in a dead faint, and it was some time before any word could be got from him.

By then they had something else to look at. The lantern must have broken at the bottom, and the light in it caught upon dry leaves and rubbish that lay there for in a few minutes a dense smoke began to come up, and then flame; and, to be short, the tree was in a blaze. The bystanders made a ring at some yards' distance, and Sir William and the bishop sent men to get what weapons and tools they could; for, clearly, whatever might be using the tree as its lair would be forced out by the fire.

So it was. First, at the fork, they saw a round body covered with fire—the size of a man's head—appear very suddenly, then seem to collapse and fall back. This, five or six times; then a similar ball leapt into the air and fell on the grass, where after a moment it lay still. The bishop went as near as he dared to it, and saw—what but the remains of an enormous spider, veinous and seared! And, as the fire burned lower down, more terrible bodies like this began to break out from the trunk, and it was seen that these were covered with greyish hair.

All that day the ash burned, and until it fell to pieces the men stood about it, and from time to time killed the brutes as they darted out. At last there was a long interval when none appeared, and they cautiously closed in and examined the roots of the tree.

'They found,' says the Bishop of Kilmore, 'below it a rounded hollow place in the earth, wherein were two or three bodies of these creatures that had plainly been smothered by the smoke; and, what is to me more curious, at the side of this den, against the wall, was crouching the anatomy or skeleton of a human being, with the skin dried upon the bones, having some remains of black hair, which was pronounced by those that examined it to be undoubtedly the body of a woman, and clearly dead for a period of fifty years.'

The Tomb of Sarah

F. G. LORING

M y father was the head of a celebrated firm of church restorers and decorators about sixty years ago. He took a keen interest in his work, and made an especial study of any old legends or family histories that came under his observation. He was necessarily very well read and thoroughly well posted in all questions of folklore and medieval legend. As he kept a careful record of every case he investigated the manuscripts he left at his death have a special interest. From amongst them I have selected the following, as being a particularly weird and extraordinary experience. In presenting it to the public I feel it is superfluous to apologize for its supernatural character.

MY FATHER'S DIARY

1841. *June 17th*. Received a commission from my old friend

Peter Grant to enlarge and restore the chancel of his church at Hagarstone, in the wilds of the West Country.

July 5th. Went down to Hagarstone with my head man, Somers. A very long and tiring journey.

July 7th. Got the work well started. The old church is one of special interest to the antiquarian, and I shall endeavour while restoring it to alter the existing arrangements as little as possible. One large tomb, however, must be moved bodily ten feet at least to the southward. Curiously enough, there is a somewhat forbidding inscription upon it in Latin, and I am sorry that this particular tomb should have to be moved. It stands amongst the graves of the Kenyons, an old family which has been extinct in these parts for centuries. The inscription on it runs thus:

SARAH.
1630.
FOR THE SAKE OF THE DEAD AND THE WELFARE OF THE LIVING, LET THIS SEPULCHRE REMAIN UNTOUCHED AND ITS OCCUPANT UNDISTURBED TILL THE COMING OF CHRIST.
IN THE NAME OF THE FATHER, THE SON, AND THE HOLY GHOST.

July 8th. Took counsel with Grant concerning the 'Sarah Tomb'. We are both very loath to disturb it, but the ground has sunk so beneath it that the safety of the church is in danger; thus we have no choice. However, the work shall be done as reverently as possible under our own direction.

Grant says there is a legend in the neighbourhood that it is the tomb of the last of the Kenyons, the evil Countess Sarah, who was murdered in 1630. She lived quite alone in the old castle, whose ruins still stand three miles from here on the road to Bristol. Her reputation was an evil one even for those days. She was a witch or were-woman, the only companion of her solitude being a familiar in the shape of a huge Asiatic wolf. This creature was reputed to seize upon children, or failing these, sheep and other small animals, and convey them to the castle, where the countess used to suck their blood. It was popularly supposed that she could never be killed. This, however, proved a fallacy, since she was strangled one day by a mad peasant woman who had lost two children, she declaring that they had both been seized and carried off by the countess's familiar. This is a very interesting story, since it points to a local superstition very similar to that of the vampire, existing in Slavonic and Hungarian Europe.

The tomb is built of black marble, surmounted by an enormous slab of the same material. On the slab is a magnificent group of figures. A young and handsome woman reclines upon a couch; round her neck is a piece of rope, the end of which she holds in her hand. At her side is a gigantic dog with bared fangs and lolling tongue. The face of the reclining figure is a cruel one: the corners of the mouth are curiously lifted, showing the sharp points of long canine or dog teeth. The whole group, though magnificently executed, leaves a most unpleasant sensation.

If we move the tomb it will have to be done in two pieces, the covering slab first and then the tomb proper. We have decided to remove the covering tomorrow.

July 9th. 6 p.m. A very strange day.

By noon everything was ready for lifting off the covering stone, and after the men's dinner we started the jacks and pulleys. The slab lifted easily enough, though it fitted closely into its seat and was further secured by some sort of mortar or putty, which must have kept the interior perfectly air-tight.

None of us were prepared for the horrible rush of foul, mouldy air that escaped as the cover lifted clear of its seating. And the contents that gradually came into view were more startling still. There lay the fully dressed body of a woman, wizened and shrunk and ghastly pale as if from starvation. Round her neck was a loose cord, and, judging by the scars still visible, the story of death by strangulation was true enough.

The most horrible part, however, was the extraordinary freshness of the body. Except for the appearance of starvation, life might have been only just extinct. The flesh was soft and white, the eyes were wide open and seemed to stare at us with a fearful understanding in them. The body itself lay on mould, without any pretence to coffin or shell.

For several moments we gazed with horrible curiosity, and then it became too much for my workmen, who implored us to replace the covering slab. That, of course, we would not do; but

I set the carpenters to work at once to make a temporary cover while we moved the tomb to its new position. This is a long job, and will take two or three days at least.

July 9th. 9 p.m. Just at sunset we were startled by the howling of, seemingly, every dog in the village. It lasted for ten minutes or a quarter of an hour, and then ceased as suddenly as it began. This, and a curious mist that has risen round the church, makes me feel rather anxious about the 'Sarah Tomb'. According to the best-established traditions of the vampire-haunted countries, the disturbance of dogs or wolves at sunset is supposed to indicate the presence of one of these fiends, and local fog is always considered to be a certain sign. The vampire has the power of producing it for the purpose of concealing its movements near its hiding-place at any time.

I dare not mention or even hint my fears to the rector, for he is, not unnaturally perhaps, a rank disbeliever in many things that I know, from experience, are not only possible but even probable. I must work this out alone at first, and get his aid without his knowing in what direction he is helping me. I shall now watch till midnight at least.

10.15 p.m. As I feared and half expected. Just before ten there was another outburst of the hideous howling. It was commenced most distinctly by a particularly horrible and blood-curdling wail from the vicinity of the churchyard. The chorus lasted only a few minutes, however, and at the end of it I saw a large dark shape, like a huge dog, emerge from the fog and lope away at a rapid canter towards the open country. Assuming this to be what I fear, I shall see it return soon after midnight.

12.30 a.m. I was right. Almost as midnight struck I saw the beast returning. It stopped at the spot where the fog seemed to commence, and lifting up its head, gave tongue to that particularly horrible long-drawn wail that I had noticed as preceding the outburst earlier in the evening.

Tomorrow I shall tell the rector what I have seen; and if, as I expect, we hear of some neighbouring sheepfold having been raided, I shall get him to watch with me for this nocturnal marauder. I shall also examine the 'Sarah Tomb' for something which he may notice without any previous hint from me.

July 10th. I found the workmen this morning much disturbed in mind about the howling of the dogs. 'We doan't like it, zur,' one of them said to me—'we doan't like it; there was summat abroad last night that was unholy.' They were still more uncomfortable when the news came round that a large dog had made a raid upon a flock of sheep, scattering them far and wide, and leaving three of them dead with torn throats in the field.

When I told the rector of what I had seen and what was being said in the village, he immediately decided that we must try and catch or at least identify the beast I had seen. 'Of course,' said he, 'it is some dog lately imported into the neighbourhood, for I know of nothing about here nearly as large as the animal you describe, though its size may be due to the deceptive moonlight.'

This afternoon I asked the rector, as a favour, to assist me in lifting the temporary cover that was on the tomb, giving as an excuse the reason that I wished to obtain a portion of the curious mortar with which it had been sealed. After a slight demur he consented, and we raised the lid. If the sight that met our eyes gave me a shock, at least it appalled Grant.

'Great God!' he exclaimed; 'the woman is alive!'

And so it seemed for a moment. The corpse had lost much of its starved appearance and looked hideously fresh and alive. It was still wrinkled and shrunken, but the lips were firm, and of the rich red hue of health. The eyes, if possible, were more appalling than ever, though fixed and staring. At one corner of the mouth I thought I noticed a slight dark-coloured froth, but I said nothing about it then.

'Take your piece of mortar, Harry,' gasped Grant, 'and let us shut the tomb again. God help me! Parson though I am, such dead faces frighten me!'

Nor was I sorry to hide that terrible face again; but I got my bit of mortar, and I have advanced a step towards the solution of the mystery.

This afternoon the tomb was moved several feet towards its new position, but it will be two or three days yet before we shall be ready to replace the slab.

10.15 p.m. Again the same howling at sunset, the same fog enveloping the church, and at ten o'clock the same great beast slipping silently out into the open country. I must get the rector's help and watch for its return. But precautions we must take, for if things are as I believe, we take our lives in our hands when we venture out into the night to waylay the—vampire.

Why not admit it at once? For that the beast I have seen is the vampire of that evil thing in the tomb I can have no reasonable doubt.

Not yet come to its full strength, thank Heaven! after the starvation of nearly two centuries, for at present it can only maraud as wolf apparently. But, in a day or two, when full power returns, that dreadful woman in new strength and beauty will be able to leave her refuge. Then it would not be sheep merely that would satisfy her disgusting lust for blood, but victims that would yield their life-blood without a murmur to her caressing touch—victims that, dying of her foul embrace, themselves must become vampires in their turn to prey on others.

Mercifully my knowledge gives me a safeguard; for that little piece of mortar that I rescued today from the tomb contains a portion of the Sacred Host, and who holds it, humbly and firmly believing in its virtue, may pass safely through such an ordeal as I intend to submit myself and the rector to tonight.

12.30 a.m. Our adventure is over for the present, and we are back safe.

After writing the last entry recorded above, I went off to find Grant and tell him that the marauder was out on the prowl again. 'But, Grant,' I said, 'before we start out tonight I must insist that you will let me prosecute this affair in my own way; you must promise to put yourself completely under my orders, without asking any questions as to the why and wherefore.'

After a little demur, and some excusable chaff on his part at the serious view I was taking of what he called a 'dog hunt', he gave me his promise. I then told him that we were to watch tonight and try and track the mysterious beast, but not to interfere with it in any way. I think, in spite of his jests, that I impressed him with the fact that there might be, after all, good reason for my precautions.

It was just after eleven when we stepped out into the still night.

Our first move was to try and penetrate the dense fog round the church, but there was something so chilly about it, and a faint smell so disgustingly rank and loathsome, that neither our nerves nor our stomachs were proof against it. Instead, we stationed ourselves in the dark shadow of a yew tree that commanded a good view of the wicket entrance to the churchyard.

At midnight the howling of the dogs began again, and in a few minutes we saw a large grey shape, with green eyes shining like lamps, shamble swiftly down the path towards us.

The rector started forward, but I laid a firm hand upon his arm and whispered a warning 'Remember!' Then we both stood very still and watched as the great beast cantered swiftly by. It was real enough, for we could hear the clicking of its nails on the stone flags. It passed within a few yards of us, and seemed to be nothing more nor less than a great grey wolf, thin and gaunt, with bristling hair and dripping jaws. It stopped where the mist commenced, and turned round. It was truly a horrible sight, and made one's blood run cold. The eyes burnt like fires, the upper lip was snarling and raised, showing the great canine teeth, while round the mouth clung and dripped a dark-coloured froth.

It raised its head and gave tongue to its long wailing howl, which was answered from afar by the village dogs. After standing for a few moments it turned and disappeared into the thickest part of the fog.

Very shortly afterwards the atmosphere began to clear, and within ten minutes the mist was all gone, the dogs in the village were silent, and the night seemed to reassume its normal aspect. We examined the spot where the beast had been standing and found, plainly enough upon the stone flags, dark spots of froth and saliva.

'Well, rector,' I said, 'will you admit now, in view of the things you have seen today, in consideration of the legend, the woman in the tomb, the fog, the howling dogs, and, last but not least, the mysterious beast you have seen so close, that there is something not quite normal in it all? Will you put yourself unreservedly in my hands and help me, *whatever I may do*, to first make assurance doubly sure, and finally take the necessary steps for putting an end to this horror of the night?' I saw that the uncanny influence of the night was strong upon him, and wished to impress it as much as possible.

'Needs must,' he replied, 'when the Devil drives: and in the face of what I have seen I must believe that some unholy forces are at work. Yet, how can they work in the sacred precincts of a church? Shall we not call rather upon Heaven to assist us in our need.'

'Grant,' I said solemnly, 'that we must do, each in his own way. God helps those who help themselves, and by His help and the light of my knowledge we must fight this battle for Him and the poor lost soul within.'

We then returned to the rectory and to our rooms, though I have sat up to write this account while the scene is fresh in my mind.

July 11th. Found the workmen again very much disturbed in their minds, and full of a strange dog that had been seen during the night by several people, who had hunted it. Farmer Stotman, who had been watching his sheep (the same flock that had been raided the night before), had surprised it over a fresh carcass and tried to drive it off, but its size and fierceness so alarmed him that he had beaten a hasty retreat for a gun. When he returned the animal was gone, though he found that three more sheep from his flock were dead and torn.

The 'Sarah Tomb' was moved today to its new position; but it was a long, heavy business, and there was not time to replace the covering slab. For this I was glad, as in the prosaic light of day the rector almost disbelieves the events of the night, and is prepared to think everything to have been magnified and distorted by our imagination.

As, however, I could not possibly proceed with my war of extermination against this foul thing without assistance, and as there is nobody else I can rely upon, I appealed to him for one more night—to convince him that it was no delusion, but a ghastly, horrible truth, which must be fought and conquered for our own sakes, as well as that of all those living in the neighbourhood.

'Put yourself in my hands, rector,' I said, 'for tonight at least. Let us take those precautions which my study of the subject tells me are the right ones. Tonight you and I must watch in the church; and I feel assured that tomorrow you will be as convinced as I am, and be equally prepared to take those awful steps which I know to be proper, and I must warn you that we shall find a more startling change in the body lying there than you noticed yesterday.'

My words came true; for on raising the wooden cover once

more the rank stench of a slaughterhouse arose, making us feel positively sick. There lay the vampire, but how changed from the starved and shrunken corpse we saw two days ago for the first time! The wrinkles had almost disappeared, the flesh was firm and full, the crimson lips grinned horribly over the long pointed teeth, and a distinct smear of blood had trickled down one corner of the mouth. We set our teeth, however, and hardened our hearts. Then we replaced the cover and put what we had collected into a safe place in the vestry. Yet even now Grant could not believe that there was any real or pressing danger concealed in that awful tomb, as he raised strenuous objections to any apparent desecration of the body without further proof. This he shall have tonight. God grant that I am not taking too much on myself! If there is any truth in old legends it would be easy enough to destroy the vampire now; but Grant will not have it.

I hope for the best of this night's work, but the danger in waiting is very great.

6 p.m. I have prepared everything: the sharp knives, the pointed stake, fresh garlic, and the wild dog-roses. All these I have taken and concealed in the vestry, where we can get at them when our solemn vigil commences.

If either or both of us die with our fearful task undone, let those reading my record see that this is done. I lay it upon them as a solemn obligation. 'That the vampire be pierced through the heart with the stake, then let the Burial Service be read over the poor clay at last released from its doom. Thus shall the vampire cease to be, and a lost soul rest.'

July 12th. All is over. After the most terrible night of watching and horror one vampire at least will trouble the world no more. But how thankful should we be to a merciful Providence that that awful tomb was not disturbed by anyone not having the knowledge necessary to deal with its dreadful occupant! I write this with no feelings of self-complacency, but simply with a great gratitude for the years of study I have been able to devote to this special subject.

And now to my tale.

Just before sunset last night the rector and I locked ourselves into the church, and took up our position in the pulpit. It was one of those pulpits, to be found in some churches, which is entered from the vestry, the preacher appearing at a good height through an arched opening in the wall. This gave us a sense of security (which we felt we needed), a good view of the interior, and direct access to the implements which I had concealed in the vestry.

The sun set and the twilight gradually deepened and faded. There was, so far, no sign of the usual fog, nor any howling of the dogs. At nine o'clock the moon rose, and her pale light gradually flooded the aisles, and still no sign of any kind from the 'Sarah Tomb'. The rector had asked me several times what he might expect, but I was determined that no words or thought of mine should influence him, and that he should be convinced by his own senses alone.

By half-past ten we were both getting very tired, and I began to think that perhaps after all we should see nothing that night. However, soon after eleven we observed a light mist rising from the 'Sarah Tomb'. It seemed to scintillate and sparkle as it rose, and curled in a sort of pillar or spiral.

I said nothing, but I heard the rector give a sort of gasp as he clutched my arm feverishly. 'Great Heaven!' he whispered, 'it is taking shape.'

And, true enough, in a very few moments we saw standing erect by the tomb the ghastly figure of the Countess Sarah!

She looked thin and haggard still, and her face was deadly white; but the crimson lips looked like a hideous gash in the pale cheeks, and her eyes glared like red coals in the gloom of the church.

It was a fearful thing to watch as she stepped unsteadily down the aisle, staggering a little as if from weakness and exhaustion. This was perhaps natural, as her body must have suffered much physically from her long incarceration, in spite of the unholy forces which kept it fresh and well.

We watched her to the door, and wondered what would happen; but it appeared to present no difficulty, for she melted through it and disappeared.

'Now, Grant,' I said, 'do you believe?'

'Yes,' he replied, 'I must. Everything is in your hands, and I will obey your commands to the letter, if you can only instruct me how to rid my poor people of this unnameable terror.'

'By God's help I will,' said I; 'but you shall be yet more convinced first, for we have a terrible work to do, and much to answer for in the future, before we leave the church again this morning. And now to work, for in its present weak state the vampire will not wander far, but may return at any time, and must not find us unprepared.'

We stepped down from the pulpit and, taking dog-roses and garlic from the vestry, proceeded to the tomb. I arrived first and, throwing off the wooden cover, cried, 'Look! it is empty!' There was nothing there! Nothing except the impress of the body in the loose damp mould!

I took the flowers and laid them in a circle round the tomb, for legend teaches us that vampires will not pass over these particular blossoms if they can avoid it.

Then, eight or ten feet away, I made a circle on the stone pavement, large enough for the rector and myself to stand in, and within the circle I placed the implements that I had brought into the church with me.

'Now,' I said, 'from this circle, which nothing unholy can step across, you shall see the vampire face to face, and see her afraid to cross that other circle of garlic and dog-roses to regain her unholy refuge. But on no account step beyond the holy place you stand in, for the vampire has a fearful strength not her own, and, like a snake, can draw her victim willingly to his own destruction.'

Now so far my work was done, and, calling the rector, we stepped into the Holy Circle to await the vampire's return.

Nor was this long delayed. Presently a damp, cold odour seemed to pervade the church, which made our hair bristle and flesh to creep. And then, down the aisle with noiseless feet came That which we watched for.

I heard the rector mutter a prayer, and I held him tightly by the arm, for he was shivering violently.

Long before we could distinguish the features we saw the glowing eyes and the crimson sensual mouth. She went straight to her tomb, but stopped short when she encountered my flowers. She walked right round the tomb seeking a place to enter, and as she walked she saw us. A spasm of diabolical hate and fury passed over her face; but it quickly vanished, and a smile of love, more devilish still, took its place. She stretched out her arms towards us. Then we saw that round her mouth gathered a bloody froth, and from under her lips long pointed teeth gleamed and champed.

She spoke: a soft soothing voice, a voice that carried a spell with it, and affected us both strangely, particularly the rector. I wished to test as far as possible, without endangering our lives, the vampire's power. Her voice had a soporific effect, which I resisted easily enough, but which seemed to throw the rector into a sort of trance. More than this: it seemed to compel him to her in spite of his efforts to resist.

'Come!' she said— 'come! I give sleep and peace—sleep and peace—sleep and peace.'

She advanced a little towards us; but not far, for I noted that the Sacred Circle seemed to keep her back like an iron hand.

My companion seemed to become demoralized and spellbound. He tried to step forward and, finding me detain him, whispered, 'Harry, let go! I must go! She is calling me! I must! I must! Oh, help me! help me!' And he began to struggle.

It was time to finish.

'Grant!' I cried, in a loud, firm voice, 'in the name of all that you hold sacred, have done and play the man!' He shuddered violently and gasped, 'Where am I?' Then he remembered, and clung to me convulsively for a moment.

At this a look of damnable hate changed the smiling face before us, and with a sort of shriek she staggered back.

'Back!' I cried: 'back to your unholy tomb! No longer shall you molest the suffering world! Your end is near.'

It was fear that now showed itself in her beautiful face (for it was beautiful in spite of its horror) as she shrank back, back and over the circlet of flowers, shivering as she did so. At last, with a low mournful cry, she appeared to melt back again into her tomb.

As she did so the first gleams of the rising sun lit up the world, and I knew all danger was over for the day.

Taking Grant by the arm, I drew him with me out of the circle and led him to the tomb. There lay the vampire once more, still in her living death as we had a moment before seen her in her devilish life. But in the eyes remained that awful expression of hate, and cringing, appalling fear.

Grant was pulling himself together.

'Now,' I said, 'will you dare the last terrible act and rid the world for ever of this horror?'

'By God!' he said solemnly, 'I will. Tell me what to do.'

'Help me to lift her out of her tomb. She can harm us no more,' I replied.

With averted faces we set to our terrible task, and laid her out upon the flags.

'Now,' I said, 'read the Burial Service over the poor body, and then let us give it its release from this living hell that holds it.'

Reverently the rector read the beautiful words, and reverently I made the necessary responses. When it was over I took the stake and, without giving myself time to think, plunged it with all my strength through the heart.

As though really alive, the body for a moment writhed and kicked convulsively, and an awful heart-rending shriek woke the silent church; then all was still.

Then we lifted the poor body back; and, thank God! the consolation that legend tells is never denied to those who have to do such awful work as ours came at last. Over the face stole a great and solemn peace; the lips lost their crimson hue, the prominent sharp teeth sank back into the mouth, and for a moment we saw before us the calm, pale face of a most beautiful woman, who smiled as she slept. A few minutes more, and she faded away to dust before our eyes as we watched. We set to work and cleaned up every trace of our work, and then departed for the rectory. Most thankful were we to step out of the church, with its horrible associations, into the rosy warmth of the summer morning.

With the above end the notes in my father's diary, though a few days later this further entry occurs:

July 15th. Since the 12th everything has been quiet and as usual. We replaced and sealed up the 'Sarah Tomb' this morning. The workmen were surprised to find the body had disappeared, but took it to be the natural result of exposing it to the air.

One odd thing came to my ears today. It appears that the child of one of the villagers strayed from home the night of the 11th inst., and was found asleep in a coppice near the church, very pale and quite exhausted. There were two small marks on her throat, which have since disappeared.

What does this mean? I have, however, kept it to myself, as, now that the vampire is no more, no further danger either to that child or any other is to be apprehended. It is only those who die of the vampire's embrace that become vampires at death in their turn.

The Hirn

PHILIPPA PEARCE

This was a new motorway, and Mr Edward Edwards liked that. He liked new things—things newly designed and newly made. He drove his powerful car powerfully, just at the speed limit, eating up the miles, as the saying is—eating up as an impatient boa-constrictor might swallow its unimportant prey.

The new motorway sliced through new countryside. (Old countryside, really, but new to motorway travellers, and that was what mattered.) Open it was, with huge fields, mostly arable. Mr Edwards approved of the evident productivity.

He drove well, looking ahead at the road, keeping an eye on the rear-view mirror, and at the same time sparing casual glances towards the landscape on the right and on the left.

Something snagged in Mr Edwards's mind, suddenly: there was an unexpected and unwelcome catching of his attention, as though on some country walk a hanging bramble had caught on his sleeve, on his arm. (But he had not gone on any country walk for many years.)

He glanced sharply to his left again.

To his left the gentle rise and fall of farmland was perhaps familiar . . .

And that house . . .

That farmhouse . . .

Instantly Mr Edward Edwards had looked away from the farmhouse; but he could not prevent himself from remembering. He was driving his car as fast and as well as before, but he remembered. They say that, in the moment of drowning, a man may remember the whole of his past life, *see* it. In the moment of driving past Mortlock's, Mr Edward Edwards remembered everything, saw everything in his mind's eye, from long ago.

The farmhouse and farmlands had belonged to the Mortlocks for several generations; but in the last generation there had been no children. The heir was young Edward Edwards, from London, whose grandmother happened to have been a Mortlock.

After the funeral of his last elderly cousin, young Edward stayed on at Mortlock's to see exactly what his inheritance consisted of—and what further might be made of it. He knew nothing of farming, but already he knew about money and its uses. Already he knew what was what.

Above all, he was clever enough to know his own ignorance. He certainly did not intend—at least, at first—to try farming on his own. He might, however, put in an experienced farm manager—but keep an eye on him, too.

He suspected that a good deal could be done to improve on Mortlock methods of farming. He understood, for instance, that up-to-date farmers were grubbing up hedges to make larger, more economic fields. That was an obvious increase in efficiency. No land should be wasted; every acre—only he thought modernly in hectares—ought to be utilized. Total efficiency would be his aim—or rather, the aim of his farm manager.

Meanwhile, he had just a farm foreman: old Bill Hayes.

Bill Hayes was old only in the dialect of the countryside; in actuality, he was young middle-aged. That local inaccuracy of speech annoyed Edward Edwards. And, anyway, although Bill Hayes was not old in age, young Edward suspected him of being old in ideas.

In the company of his farm foreman, young Edward tramped purposefully over his fields, trying to understand what he saw, and to assess its value. Often, of course, he was baffled; then Bill Hayes would do his best to explain. Sometimes young Edward was satisfied. Sometimes, however, he made a suggestion or a criticism, which Bill Hayes would invariably show to be impractical, even foolish.

Edward Edwards began to dislike old Bill Hayes.

The only time he was certain of his opinion against the foreman's was over the Hirn. This was an area of trees, using up about a third of a hectare of land, in the middle of one of the best fields.

'What is it?' asked young Edward Edwards, staring across the stubbled earth to that secretive-looking clump of trees.

And old Bill had answered: 'It's Hirn.'

'Just some trees?'

'Well, there's water too, in the middle,' said old Bill. 'You could call it a pond.'

'But what's the point of it?'

And old Bill Hayes had repeated: 'It's Hirn.'

Somehow his careless omission, twice, of the 'the' that so obviously should have been there, irritated young Edward. Again, there was that stupid suggestion of dialect, old worldness, and the rest. 'Well,' he said, 'the Hirn will have to justify its existence, if it's to remain. Otherwise, it goes.'

'Goes?'

'The land must be reclaimed for better use.'

'Better use? For Hirn?'

Young Edward thought: the fellow has an echo-chamber where his brains should be! Aloud, he said: 'If we get rid of the trees, and fill in this pond-place, then we can cultivate the land with the rest of the field.'

'I shouldn't do that, sir.'

'Why not?'

Old Bill Hayes did not answer.

'What's so special about the Hirn, then?'

Bill Hayes said: 'Well, after all, it is Hirn . . .'

Young Edward could get no further than that. But at least this senseless conversation made plain to him that he must get rid of old Bill Hayes as soon as possible. He needed a thoroughly rational, modern-minded farm manager: that was certain. This business of the Hirn was typical of what must have been going on, unchecked, during the Mortlock years.

Young Edward was pretty certain that the Hirn must be dealt with—and the sooner the better, of course. But he was not impulsive, not foolhardy. He would examine the site carefully for himself—and by himself—before coming to a decision. After all, there might even be valuable timber among those trees. (He was pleased with himself for the thought: surely, he was already learning.)

So the next day he set off alone in his car—not at all a car of the make, age, or condition that, in later years, he would care to have been seen driving. He knew the nearest point of access to the Hirn: a side road, along which had been built a line of Council houses. Just beyond the last house, on the same side, was a field-gate, and by this he parked. Through the gate, in the distance, he could already see the Hirn.

He climbed the gate and set off across the fields, passing by the side of the back garden of the last Council house. A woman was pegging out her washing, and a toddler played about beside the washing-basket. The toddler stopped playing to stare; but his mother went on with her work. Yet young Edward felt sure that she, too, was watching him. No wonder, perhaps—this little colony of houses was remote from most comings and goings.

A little later, as he was crossing the furrows, he looked back, to mark the gateway where he had left the car, and to see whether—yes, the two in the garden were now both openly staring after him. The woman held the child in her arms; and an old man had also come out of the house next door. He stood just the other side of the hedge from the woman and child, staring in the same direction.

Edward Edwards reached the Hirn. Even he could see that the woodland had been disgracefully neglected: no one had laid a finger on it for many, many years—perhaps ever, it seemed. The trees grew all anyhow: some strangled by ivy; some age-decayed and falling; some crippled by the fall of others; some young, but stunted and deformed in the struggle upwards to the sunlight. The space between the trees was dense with undergrowth.

It was very still, but no doubt there would be birds and other wild creatures. Young Edward peered about him. He could see no movement at all; but he supposed that beady bird-eyes would be watching him.

He began to push his way through the undergrowth between the trees, to find the water of which Bill Hayes had spoken.

He came to a small clearing—so it seemed—among the trees: open, green, and almost eerily even. Absolutely flat. He hesitated at the edge of the clearing, and then, with a shock, realized that this was the water. Mantled by some over-spreading tiny plant life, it had seemed to him to be solid, turfy land. He had almost fallen into the pond—almost walked into it.

There was no knowing how deep the water was.

The water was unmoving, except perhaps at its edges, where he thought he saw, out of the corner of his eye, a slight stirring. Perhaps tadpoles? But was this the season for tadpoles? He tried to remember; but he had never been much of a tadpole boy, even with the few opportunities that London offered. He had always hated that dark wriggliness.

He decided to complete his examination by walking round the edge of the pond. This turned out to be difficult, because of the thickly growing vegetation. At one place a bush leant in a straggly way over the water; it bore clusters of tiny, dark-purple berries. He thought that these must be elderberries, and he knew you could eat elderberries. He stretched out a hand to pick some, and then thought that perhaps these were not elderberries; perhaps another kind of fruit; perhaps poisonous. He drew his hand back sharply. He felt endangered.

And then he saw the amazing oak. The trunk must have been at least two metres across at its base, but the tree was quite hollow, with some other younger tree boldly growing up in the middle of it. All the same, the oak was not dead: from its crust of bark twigs and leaves had spurted. And at some time someone—apparently to keep this shell of a tree from falling apart—had put a steel cable round it.

'Pointless,' said young Edward to himself. Because of the

elderberries—if they had been elderberries—he had felt afraid, and that still angered him. Now the sight of the giant oak, whose collapse was thus futilely delayed, angered him even more.

He pushed his way out of the little piece of woodland to its far side and the open field beyond. From there the Council houses were not visible. The Hirn lay between.

The shortest way back to the field-gate and his car would have been by the path his pushing and trampling had already made through the woodland. But he decided not to re-enter the Hirn. He preferred to take the long way round the outside, until he was in view of the houses, the gate, the car.

When he could see the Council houses, he could see that the woman and child were still in their garden; also the old man in his. When they saw him coming, they went indoors.

'I don't know what they thought they were going to see,' young Edward said to himself resentfully. 'Something—oh, *very* extraordinary, no doubt!'

He went straight back to the car, and then home. His examination of the Hirn had been quick but thorough enough. There had been nothing much to see; and, frankly, he did not like the place.

The next day he tackled old Bill Hayes and told him that the Hirn must be obliterated. He did not use the word, but it was in his mind as he gave the order. After all, he was owner and master.

Old Bill Hayes looked at him: 'But it's Hirn,' he said.

'So you mentioned before,' said young Edward, knowing that this sarcasm would be wasted on Bill's dullness. 'All the same, see that what I want is done.'

Old Bill Hayes made no further objection; but neither did he do anything in the days that followed.

Then, realizing that his wishes had been ignored, Edward gave the order again.

Again, nothing happened.

This time, his blood up, young Edward acted for himself, without consulting or even informing old Bill Hayes. He made the right enquiries and was able to arrange for an outside firm to do the clearance job. They said it would take several days. They would start by cutting down all the trees. The timber—

valueless, of course—and the brushwood would then be cleared. Remaining tree-stumps and roots must all be grubbed up; otherwise they would grow again, even more strongly. Finally, the pond would be filled in and the whole site levelled.

In only a short time, all trace of the Hirn would have disappeared.

On the first day of the operation, young Edward Edwards had a morning appointment with the manager of the local bank where the Mortlocks had always done business. There were financial matters still to be sorted out. But, on top of these, the manager annoyed young Edward with unwanted advice. He strongly urged him not to take on the Mortlock farm on his own account, even with a farm manager. It would be more sensible (the bank manager said) to sell the farm and farmhouse, and use the money in some business which he was more likely fully to understand.

Young Edward was furious.

His fury lasted into the afternoon, when he decided that he was in just the mood to inspect the destruction of the Hirn. Besides, he somehow felt that he ought to be there—perhaps as a witness to the execution.

He drove his car to the same place as before, and set off again across the fields. It was easy to see where the gang had been before him, with their heavily loaded vehicles, and he could already see where they had been at work: the treed area of the Hirn was now only about a tenth of its original size. The other nine-tenths had been roughly cleared, leaving freshly cut tree-stumps sticking up everywhere like jagged teeth.

The gang themselves had gone home. He was disappointed—and disapproving—that they had chosen to stop work so early.

Once, before he reached what was left of the Hirn, young Edward looked back over the fields to the Council houses. No one at all in the gardens. No lights yet in any windows, as there would be soon; but he was aware of something—a pallor behind a window-glass: a face looking out in his direction. From more than one window he fancied that they watched him.

He was soon picking his way among the many tree-stumps, making for the few trees that were left standing near the pond. The dying oak had been left standing. It survived. He stared at it. Unwillingly he came to the decision that he wanted to touch it. He went right up to it and laid the flat of his hand against the bark. For the first time it occurred to him to wonder how old the tree might be. People said that oaks could live for hundreds of years . . . hundreds and hundreds of years . . .

He decided that he had seen enough of the Hirn. He turned away from the oak, to get out of this tiny remnant of woodland. Tiny it might be, but it was thick—thicker than he had noticed on his coming. He had to push his way through the under-growth—perhaps because this was not the way he had come, but a new way. Certainly it had been much easier for him to reach the oak than, now, it was for him to get away from it.

The end of the afternoon was coming; the light was failing.

He came to the pond. The water looked almost black now. To his surprise he saw that there were still trees and bushes crowding the banks round it: he had thought, as he came over the fields, that they had been cut down.

He turned away from the water in the direction—he thought—of the Council houses and his parked car. He must have made a mistake, however, for he re-entered untouched woodland again.

He was angered at how long it was taking him to get out of this wretched grove of trees.

He came to the oak again, and turned from it abruptly to struggle on through the undergrowth in the direction he supposed to be the right one. The only sound was the sound of his crashing about and his own heavy breathing; and then he thought—or perhaps he imagined?—he was hearing something else. He stopped to listen carefully . . .

(Driving fast along the motorway, Mr Edwards remembered standing still to listen so carefully, so very carefully. As he drove, his hands tightened on the driving-wheel until his knuckles whitened . . .)

Young Edward Edwards listened . . .

It was very quiet. Everywhere round him was now still and very, very quiet. But, all the same, he thought there was something—not a sound that began and ended, but a sound that was there, as the wood was there. The sound enclosed him, as the wood enclosed him.

The sound was of someone trying not to laugh—of someone privately amused—quietly and maliciously amused.

Young Edward made a rush forward, and reached the pond again.

He stood there, and the sound was there with him, all around him. He stared at the blackness of the water until he could feel his eyes beginning to trick him. He watched the water, and the water seemed to watch him. The surface of the blackness seemed to shiver, to shudder; the edges of the water seemed to crinkle. The mantle of black on the surface of the water seemed to be gathering itself up, as a woman's garments are gathered, before the woman herself rises . . .

(Along the motorway Mr Edwards drove fast, trying to think of nothing but the motorway; but he had to remember . . .)

Young Edward ran; he was trying to run; he was trying to escape. The sound was still round him; and round him now, everywhere, trees stood in his way and the undergrowth spread wide to catch him. They all baited him, for someone's private amusement. He fought to run: a bramble snagged in his sleeve, and then tried to drag the coat from his back; an elder branch whipped him across the face; a sly tree-root tripped him.

He tripped. He was falling.

He knew that he was falling among tall trees and thickets of undergrowth; and that he was lost—forever lost! He gave a long scream, but a blow on the head finished the scream, and also finished young Edward Edwards for the time being.

In the Council houses they heard the long scream that suddenly stopped, and a little party set off hurriedly to find young Mr Edwards. They had been waiting for something to happen. They were not callous people, only very fearful; otherwise they might have gone earlier.

They found him lying among the tree-stumps of the cleared part of the woodland. He had fallen head-first on to one of them. Later, in hospital, he was told that he had been very lucky: he might so easily have split his whole head open on that jagged tree-stump. Killed himself.

And later still, in London (where he had insisted on going, straight from the hospital), he had instructed the bank to arrange for the immediate sale of Mortlock's, farmhouse and farm, the lot. That had been done, most profitably, and he had never seen the place again—until today, from the motorway.

As he drove, he ventured another quick glance to his left: the farmhouse was no longer in sight. His spirits lifted. These must still be Mortlock fields, but they would soon be passed, too.

Then he saw the Council houses, and recognized them . . .

Then the big field . . .

Then, in the middle, green and flourishing, a coppice of trees . . .

He had been warned that, unless they were grubbed up by the roots, the tree-stumps would sprout and grow even more strongly. Yes, they had grown; and now, as once before, thick woodland hid from sight that mantled water. And he began to think he heard—borne on some unlikely wind—the faintest sound of unkind laughter.

Mr Edwards brought his gaze back strictly to the motorway ahead, turned the car radio on to full volume, accelerated well over the speed limit, and so passed beyond further sight of the trees that were Hirn.

He put view and sound, and remembrance of both, behind him for good. He had made up his mind, for good: he would not drive this way again. There were always other roads, and other modes of travel—rail, air. He would never use this motorway again.

He never did.

The Baby-sitter

ALISON PRINCE

Nigel's mother came into his bedroom to kiss him goodnight. She was wearing a long dress and smelt beautiful.

'You will be good, won't you?' she said. 'Mr Pope is a dear old man—and it was so sweet of him to offer to baby-sit.'

'I don't like him much,' said Nigel. 'He squashes caterpillars with his fingers.'

Nigel's mother laughed. 'You never know,' she said, 'it may be kinder than using these chemical sprays. And he is a wonderful gardener.'

'Why couldn't Aunty Betty come?' asked Nigel, frowning.

'I told you,' said his mother patiently. 'Aunty Betty's ill. And Mr Pope has offered to baby-sit ever so many times—he really loves children, he says, and never had any of his own. And he does like a warm fire to sit by, poor old chap.'

'Come on, Joyce!' shouted Nigel's father from the hall. 'We'll be late!'

'Coming!' she called back. She bent and kissed Nigel again, then tucked him in and switched off the main light, leaving the bedside lamp. She touched the tip of his nose lightly with her forefinger and said, 'Be good!' Then she went out.

'Tell him I want a story!' Nigel shouted after her.

Doors banged and Nigel heard the car start and drive away. Suddenly he felt very lonely. He pulled the bedclothes up to his chin and stared out at the shadowed bedroom. He could imagine exactly what he looked like; the pitifully small face on the white pillow, the tousled fair hair and the blue eyes brimming with tears. And nobody had bothered to read him a story. Nigel was so carried away by the pathos of this picture that he did in fact begin to cry a little.

The sitting-room door opened. Mr Pope came out and started to climb the stairs, his footsteps as slow and measured as they were when he plodded down the garden path with a bundle of rose trimmings for the bonfire. Why did he never wear gloves? When he came in for his cup of tea his hands were often criss-crossed with bleeding scratches.

Mr Pope opened the bedroom door. Nigel rubbed his eyes on the sleeve of his pyjamas but Mr Pope took no notice of the boy's pathetic state. 'Your mother tells me you want a story,' he announced. Then he closed the door behind him.

Nigel sniffed. 'Yes, please,' he said.

Mr Pope smiled slowly. Everything he did was very slow—stirring his tea, filling his pipe, pushing the lawnmower. 'I'm glad about that,' he said. 'Because I've been thinking for a long time about a story I'd like to tell you.'

'You could have told me in the garden,' said Nigel.

Mr Pope shook his head. 'Oh, no,' he said. 'Oh dear, no. This is a bedtime story. I've had it saved up. Sooner or later, I thought, his Aunty Betty will be ill. Then they'll ask me to baby-sit. I've offered enough times.'

He brought a chair to Nigel's bedside and sat down, his scarred hands spread on his knees. Nigel stared up at him, fascinated and slightly afraid. Mr Pope's face never quite seemed to go with the big, rough hands. It was a hollow face, almost, Nigel thought, like Mr Punch from the Punch and Judy show at the seaside. The cheek-bones stuck out boldly but underneath them the cheeks fell away in deep hollows that ended in a craggy jaw and a thin, scrawny neck. When Mr Pope smiled his mouth was full of china-white teeth that seemed much too big—but the strangest thing about him was his eyes.

Mr Pope's eyes were very pale blue and he never seemed to blink. He gazed ahead of him with an unwavering, pink-rimmed stare which never quite fixed on the thing he was looking at. When he regarded Nigel his eyes seemed to be looking through him, so that Nigel sometimes glanced over his shoulder to see if the real object of Mr Pope's attention was somewhere behind him.

Tonight, Mr Pope's eyes were as unblinking as ever and as Nigel stared up at him he could see the tiny network of veins which threaded the whites of the eyes, surrounding the sky blue circles of the irises with wriggly red lines. Mr Pope seemed aware of this scrutiny for he said, looking through Nigel at the wall:

'You've got blue eyes, boy. Like me.'

'Yes,' said Nigel huskily.

Mr Pope nodded. 'That's good. Yes, that's all to the good.'

'What about this story?' demanded Nigel.

'I'm coming to it,' said Mr Pope, 'as you'll see in a minute. Now, this is a true story, boy, every word of it. Afterwards, you must never think to yourself that I made it up. This is the first time I've ever told this story, and I shall never tell it again, not to a living soul. This is your story, boy, just for you.'

'Thank you!' said Nigel.

'Yes,' Mr Pope went on, 'I've waited years for this. To find the right person.'

'And it's me?' asked Nigel, pleased.

'It's you,' agreed Mr Pope.

'What's it called?' asked Nigel.

Mr Pope thought. 'I never gave it a name,' he said, 'but I suppose I'd call it, "Hacky Basham's Glass Eye".'

Nigel laughed delightedly and said, 'What a funny name!'

Mr Pope didn't laugh. 'Hacky Basham,' he said, 'got his name because he coughed. Terrible hacking cough it was. That's why we called him Hacky—you know how kids make up names for people.'

'Oh, yes,' said Nigel. 'we call our teacher Bunny because her teeth stick out.'

'Hacky seemed an old man to us kids,' Mr Pope continued, 'though I dare say he wasn't much above forty, not at first. He'd been gassed in the First World War, you see, boy, and that had ruined him. His hair turned white and he never hardly worked again through having such a cough. And he lost his eye.'

'How awful!' said Nigel. 'Did he just have a hole?'

'He did,' said Mr Pope. 'But he had a glass eye that fitted in it. Except that it didn't move, you'd never have known it wasn't real.'

'What colour was it?' enquired Nigel.

'Blue,' said Mr Pope. 'The same as the other one. Just like mine. And yours, boy.'

'Ugh!' said Nigel, fascinated.

'In those days,' Mr Pope went on, 'people didn't go in so much for baby-sitters but my mum and dad were the careful sort and if they went to the pictures they'd ask Hacky Basham to keep an eye on me. They were sorry for him, I think. "He does like a warm fire to sit by," they'd say. And they'd give him a bob or two for his trouble. But just *how* he kept an eye on me they never knew.'

'How *did* he?' asked Nigel.

'When I was tucked up in bed,' said Mr Pope, 'like you are now, boy, Hacky would come upstairs, coughing fit to bust because climbing put a strain on his lungs. And he'd come into the room and stand there, wheezing—and when he got his breath back, he'd say, "I'm going to keep an eye on you, boy." And he'd take out his glass eye and put it on the mantelpiece, right on the edge so it was looking at me. "If you're naughty," he'd say, "my eye will tell me. It always does." And he'd go off downstairs, laughing and coughing. And the eye would look at me. Even in the dark I could see it because there was a street lamp outside. The white part of the eye glowed, like a little moon.'

'How *awful*!' said Nigel.

'But that was just the beginning,' went on Mr Pope. 'One night my cousin Jack had come to stay. He was sleeping in my room on a camp-bed and I was glad of his company because my mum and dad were going out that night.'

'Did Hacky Basham come?' asked Nigel.

'He did,' said Mr Pope grimly. 'And he put his eye on the mantelpiece and went downstairs, laughing and coughing like always. Now, Jack was older than me and he said, "Here," he said, "we'll give the old boy a dose of his own medicine—frighten *him* for a change. How long does he leave that thing here?" "He comes to get it just before Mum and Dad come home," I told him, "so it's always back in his head when they come in." And I knew, boy, because I could never go to sleep with that thing watching me. "Right," says Jack, "we'll hide it." And he made me put the bedclothes over my head so I wouldn't see where he'd put it, because he said I was a coward and I'd tell Hacky where it was. And I would have done, too!'

'What happened?' breathed Nigel.

'I lay there with the sheet over my head,' said Mr Pope, 'and I listened to Jack moving about, looking for a good hiding-place. I heard him open drawers and shut them again, then he pulled the door of the wardrobe open—I know, because it squeaked. Then he shut that and I felt him stand on the end of the bed as if he was looking for a hiding-place high up—and then he opened the window. And shut it again. "You can come out now," he said to me. And he was grinning all over his face. "You haven't thrown it out in the street, have you?" I asked him—but I didn't think he had, or I'd have heard it smash on the pavement. He just laughed—but he wouldn't tell me.

'Anyway,' Mr Pope went on, 'Jack went to sleep. Snored like a pig, he did. I kept thinking about the eye, hidden somewhere and still looking at me from wherever it was, and I couldn't go to sleep. If I'd known where it was, I'd have put it back on the mantelpiece, and that's a fact. Then Hacky came upstairs. When he stopped coughing he looked on the mantelpiece, then he came over to my bed. "Where is it?" he whispered. I told him I didn't know, and I felt as if we'd done a dreadful thing. He bent over my bed with his mouth right close to my ear. "Whoever took it," he said, "will come to a bad end, very soon. But you, my boy—I'll keep an eye on you for ever."'

'What did he mean?' asked Nigel.

'Don't rush me, boy,' said Mr Pope deliberately. 'I'm telling you, aren't I? Next morning, Jack looked outside for the eye. There was a window-box on our sill—my mum was keen on flowers, see, but we didn't have a garden so she had to make do with window-boxes. And Jack had put the eye in there, wedged in the earth among the petunias. But it had gone. It couldn't have slipped out, because the earth was lower than the edges of the box. And it was too big for a bird to pick up—but it wasn't there. We both looked.'

'How odd!' said Nigel.

Mr Pope ignored him. 'When my cousin Jack was going home that morning,' he went on, 'he slipped on the wet road and fell under a tram. Killed him stone dead.'

'No!' gasped Nigel.

'Yes,' said Mr Pope. 'And that night, when I went to bed, the eye was on my mantelpiece.' He held up his hand as if to ward off any questions. 'Hacky Basham hadn't been to the house. He never came again. An infection set in that very day in the eye socket, and went through to his brain and killed him.'

'It's funny, isn't it?' said Nigel, trying to sound amused.

'Funny? Yes, I suppose you might call it funny.' Mr Pope stared through Nigel again with his pale blue eyes. 'I was *haunted*, boy. I've been haunted from that day to this.'

'What d'you mean?' asked Nigel nervously.

'Hacky Basham's glass eye never left me from that day onwards,' said Mr Pope. 'It was always there, looking at me. I never knew where it would be. If I took out my sandwiches when I went fishing there it was in the package, looking like a hard-boiled egg until it rolled over and stared up at me. It would be in my pencil case at school or in the toe of my football boot on a Saturday afternoon. If I got on a bus and felt in my pocket for the fare, the eye would be there among the pennies, waiting for me to put my hand on it.'

'But how did it *get* there?' asked Nigel.

'I wish I knew,' said Mr Pope. 'It was no good hiding it. I put it in my drawer along with my socks once when I'd asked a girl to come to the pictures with me. I bought her a packet of peanuts in the interval and when she opened them, there was the eye, staring up at her. She screamed the place down. She dropped the eye on the floor before she ran out of the cinema and I hoped that was the end of it. But, no. That night, it was back on my mantelpiece.'

'I don't think it's a very nice story,' said Nigel. 'I'd rather you read me one. There's some lovely books on my shelf over there.'

'But it's a special story, Nigel,' said Mr Pope, gazing at him with the fish-cold blue eyes. It was the first time he had called Nigel by his name and there was something oddly menacing in it.

'I don't like it,' said Nigel.

'That doesn't matter,' said Mr Pope. As if reminiscing to himself, he went on, 'Yes, the eye ruined my life. I never married—it frightened off every girl I met. And it lost me job after job by turning up at the wrong moment.'

'I'd have told my mother,' said Nigel stoutly. '*She'd* know what to do.'

'I tried that,' said Mr Pope. 'I held it out to her on the palm of my hand and said, "Mum, this is Mr Basham's glass eye." And she looked straight at it and said, "There's nothing there, dear." Dad couldn't see it, either. They went to a doctor about me after a bit. Thought I was nuts. I had to pretend I couldn't see it any more or they'd have put me in the mad-house.'

Nigel gulped. 'What happened?' he asked. 'In the end, I mean?'

'I don't know yet,' said Mr Pope. 'That's up to you.'

He felt in his pocket and brought something out in his closed fist. Nigel looked at the scarred knuckles and knew what they hid. 'Don't,' he said.

Mr Pope turned his hand over and opened the fingers. There on the palm lay the glass eye, the pale blue iris pointing directly at Nigel, staring at him with a hard, wide-open, black-centred stare. Tiny veins of red threaded the china-white ball, exactly like those in Mr Pope's own eyes. Nigel could not look away.

'*You* can see it, can't you, boy?' said Mr Pope.

Nigel nodded, speechless.

Mr Pope got up slowly, and put the eye on the mantelpiece. 'There,' he said with a dry chuckle. 'Now it will keep an eye on you.' Then he sighed a small, happy sigh. 'Peace at last,' he said. 'After a haunted lifetime. I'm grateful to you, boy. Grateful.'

Suddenly a spasm of violent coughing shook him. Nigel had never heard Mr Pope cough like that before. He had never heard him cough at all. It sounded as if the man's lungs were being torn into shreds, so destructive was the fit, so racking—so hacking. Mr Pope's breath rattled in his gullet as he strained

against the impossible attack, trying to drag some air into his lungs. Clutching at his throat, he fell to his knees, then on to his side on Nigel's bedroom floor. His pale blue eyes bulged, bloodshot, as a last bubbling groan escaped him. Then there was silence.

Nigel cowered in his bed, his whole body bathed in a cold sweat of terror. And the glass eye on the mantelpiece stared down at him with an implacable blue gaze.

It seemed a lifetime before Nigel heard the car come into the garage. Then he began to scream. A key scratched in the front door and footsteps ran up the stairs.

Nigel's mother gave a gasp of horror when she came into the room and saw Mr Pope lying motionless on the carpet. Even Nigel's father seemed upset as he bent over the man, looking into his wide-open eyes and feeling his wrist. It was some time before Nigel could make them listen to what he was shouting over and over again. 'The eye, Mummy—take the eye away!'

'What is it, darling? Tell Mummy,' she said, kneeling beside his bed and hugging him in trembling arms.

Nigel's father got up from his inspection of Mr Pope and stared at his son anxiously. 'Better get him into the spare room, Joyce,' he said. 'And I'll ring the police—and a doctor, I suppose, though poor old Pope is obviously dead.'

Nigel scrambled out of bed, averting his eyes from the dreadful thing on the mantelpiece, and trotted across the landing to the spare room, holding his mother's hand tightly. The unfamiliar bed felt cold and he shivered as he slipped between the sheets—but he didn't mind. At least in here he was safe.

'I'll turn the radiator on,' said his mother.

As she went across to the radiator under the window, Nigel gazed round the rather bleak little room. The fringed lamp cast odd-shaped shadows on the wall but there were no pictures or posters to break the monotony of the rose-patterned wallpaper, and no ornaments on the dressing-table or the mantelpiece— Nigel uttered a piercing scream which made his mother jump round from the radiator. She ran across to him.

'Darling, what's the matter?' she asked, bending over her son anxiously. 'Have you got a pain?'

The boy's blue eyes were staring in horror across the room,

his face contorted with fear. 'Why did you bring it in here?' he demanded incoherently. 'What for? Take it away, Mummy, *please*! Take it *away*!' His voice rose to a shriek of terror which brought his father rushing up the stairs and into the room.

'What on earth's going on?' he asked. His wife shook her head, bewildered.

Nigel pointed at the mantelpiece. 'There!' he insisted. 'Hacky Basham's glass eye—one of you must have brought it in—*take it away*!'

His parents exchanged worried looks above Nigel's head as they followed the boy's pointing hand.

'Nigel,' said his mother gently, 'there's nothing there, dear.'

The Water Woman and her Lover

RALPH PRINCE

It's an old Essequibo tale they used to tell in whispers. But even as they whispered the tale they were afraid the wind might blow their whisperings into the river where the water woman lived. They were afraid the water woman might hear their whisperings and return to haunt them as she had haunted her lover.

It's a strange story. Here it is from the beginning.

There was an old 'koker', or sluice-gate, near Parika, through which water passed to and from the Essequibo river for drainage of the land in the area. On moonlit nights a naked woman was often seen sitting near the koker, with her back to the road and her face to the river.

She was a fair-skinned woman, and she had long, black shiny hair rolling over her shoulders and down her back. Below her waist she was like a fish. When the moon was bright, especially at full moon time, you could see her sitting on the koker, combing her long, black, shiny hair. You could see very dimly just a part of her face—a side view. But if you stepped nearer to get a closer look, she would disappear. Without even turning her head to see who was coming, she would plunge into the river with a splash and vanish. They called her Water Mamma.

People used to come from Salem, Tuschen, Naamryck and other parts of the east bank of the Essequibo river to see this mysterious creature. They would wait in the bush near the koker from early morning, and watch to see her rise from the river. But no matter how closely they watched, they would never see her when she came from the water. For a long time they would wait, and watch the koker bathed in moonlight. Then suddenly, as if she had sprung from nowhere, the water woman would appear sitting near the koker, completely naked, facing the river, and combing her long black hair.

There was a strong belief among the villagers in the area that riches would come to anyone who found Water Mamma's comb or a lock of her hair. So they used to stay awake all night at the koker, and then early in the morning, even before the sun rose, they would search around where she had sat combing her hair. But they never found anything. Only the water that had drained off her body remained behind—and also a strong fishy smell.

The old people said that after looking at Water Mamma or searching near the koker for her hair and her comb, you were always left feeling haunted and afraid. They told stories of people found sleeping, as if in a trance, while walking away from the koker. They warned that if a man watched her too long, and searched for her hair and her comb too often, he would dream about her. And if the man loved her and she loved him, she would haunt him in his dreams. And that would be the end of him, they said, because she was a creature of the devil.

These warnings did not frighten the younger and more adventurous men from the villages around. They kept coming from near and far to gaze at Water Mamma. After watching her and searching for her hair and her comb, they always had that haunted, fearful feeling. And many mornings, even as they walked away from the koker, they slept, as in a trance. But still they returned, night after night, to stare in wonder at that strange, mysterious woman.

At last something happened—something the old people had always said would happen—a man fell in love with the water woman. Some say he was from Salem. Some say he came from Naamryck. Others say he hailed from Parika, not far from the koker. Where he came from is not definitely known; but it is certain that he was a young man, tall and dark and big, with broad shoulders. His name was John, and they called him Big John because of his size.

When Big John had first heard of Water Mamma, he laughed and said she was a jumbie. But as time went by, he heard so many strange things about her that he became curious. And so one moonlit night he went to the koker to look at the water woman.

He had waited for nearly an hour, and watched the moonlight shining on the koker and the river. His old doubts had returned and he was about to leave when he saw something strange, something that 'mek he head rise', as the old folks say when telling the story. He saw a naked woman sitting near the koker. A moment before, he had seen no one there. Then suddenly he saw this strange woman sitting in the moonlight and combing her long, black hair. It shone brightly in the moonlight.

Big John made a few steps towards her to see her more clearly. Then suddenly she was gone. Without even turning her head around to look at him, she plunged into the river with a big splash and vanished. Where he had seen her sitting, there was a pool of water. And there arose a strong fishy smell. A feeling of dread overcame him.

He then set out to get away from there. He tried to run but could only walk. And even as he began walking his steps were slow and his eyes were heavy with sleep. And that is the way he went home, walking and staggering, barely able to open his eyes now and then to see where he was going, walking and sleeping, as in a trance.

The next morning, when Big John awoke and remembered what he had seen and experienced the night before, he became afraid. He vowed never to go back to the koker to look at the water woman. But that night the moon rose, flooding the land in silver, glistening in the trees, sparkling on the river. He became enchanted. His thoughts turned to the riverside and the strange woman combing her long, black hair.

And so later that night he stood near the koker waiting and watching for the strange woman to appear. Just like the night before, she appeared suddenly near the koker, combing her hair in the moonlight. Big John stepped towards her, but she plunged into the river and disappeared. And once again he had that feeling of dread, followed by drowsiness as he walked home.

This went on for several nights, with Big John becoming more and more fascinated as he watched the water woman combing her hair in the moonlight. After the third night, he no longer felt afraid, and he walked in the pool of water she had left behind. Sometimes he waited until morning and searched around for locks of her hair and her comb, but he never found them.

After a few months of this waiting and watching, Big John felt sad and lost. He had fallen in love with the strange woman. But he could not get near to her. And so he stopped going to the riverside to watch her.

When the moon had gone and the dark nights came back, he began to drop her from his mind. But in another month the moon returned, flooding the land in silver, gleaming in the trees, sparkling on the river, and he remembered the water woman, and he longed to see her combing her hair again.

And on the very night when the moon returned, he had a strange dream. He saw the water woman sitting near the koker, combing her long, black hair shining in the moonlight. She sat with her back to the river and her face full towards him. As she combed her hair, she smiled at him, enchanting him with her beauty. He stepped forward to get a closer look, but she did not move. And so at last he saw her clearly, her bright eyes, her lovely face, her teeth sparkling as she smiled, and her body below her waist tapered off like a fish. She was the most beautiful creature he had ever seen.

He stretched out his hands to touch her, and she gave him her comb and said, 'Take this to remember me by.'

Then she jumped into the river and disappeared.

When he awoke the next morning, he remembered the dream. He felt happy as he told his friends what he had seen in the dream. But they were afraid for him, and they warned him:

'Is haunt she hauntin' you.'

'She goin' mek you dream an' dream till you don' know wha' to do wid yourself.'

'When she ready she goin' do wha' she like wid you.'

'Big John, you better watch yourself wid de water woman.'

'De water woman goin' haunt you to de en'.'

These warnings made Big John laugh, and he told them:

'She can' do me anyt'ing in a dream.'

But they warned him again:

'You forget 'bout de water woman, but she don' forget 'bout you.'

'Is you start it when you watch she so much at de koker.'

'Now you 'rouse she an' she want you. Da is de story now, she want you.'

Big John laughed off these warnings and told them that nothing was going to happen to him as nothing could come from a dream.

But later that day he saw something strange. It made him shiver with dread. On the floor near his bed was a comb. He could not believe his eyes. It looked very much like the comb the water woman had given to him in the dream. He wondered how a comb he had seen in a dream could get into his room.

When he told his friends about finding the comb they said:

'Is bes' for you to go 'way from here.'

'Is you start it when you watch she so much at de koker.'

That night he had another dream. In this dream he saw the water woman sitting in the moonlight. He stepped even closer to her than before, and she smiled at him.

For the first time since he had seen her, she was not combing her hair, and she had no comb in her hand. She pulled out a few strands of her hair and gave them to him and said, 'Keep these to remember me by.' And he took them in his hands and smiled at her. In another instant she was gone with a splash into the river.

The next morning Big John awoke with a smile as he remembered the dream. But as he sat up in the bed he found himself with a few strands of hair in his hands. His eyes opened wide in surprise. It was only then that he realized that he was getting caught up in something strange.

And so the dreams went on, night after night. They became like magnets drawing Big John to bed early every night, and holding him fast in sleep till morning. They no longer made him feel afraid on awakening.

In one dream, the water woman gave him a conch shell. On awakening the next morning he found sand on his bed and grains of sand in both hands. One night he dreamt that he and the water woman played along the river bank splashing each other with water. The next morning he found his bed wet, and water splashed all over the room.

Big John told his friends about these dreams, and they warned him that the water woman had him under a spell. They were right. He kept on dreaming about her night after night.

Then came his last dream. The water woman stood by the riverside holding a large bundle to her bosom. She smiled and said:

'You have my comb and strands of my hair. I have given you other little gifts to remember me by. Tonight I shall give you money to make you rich. If you keep it a secret, you will stay on earth and enjoy it. If you do not keep it a secret, you must come with me and be my lover for ever.'

She hurled the bundle to him, and then jumped into the river and was gone.

When Big John awoke the next morning, he found the floor of the room covered with tens of thousands of five-dollar bills, piled up high in heaps. It took him a long time to gather them and count them. It was a vast fortune.

Big John was too excited to keep the news about the dream and the fortune it had brought him. He went around the village and told some of his closest friends about it. When they went with him to his house and saw those great piles of money, their eyes bulged and their mouths opened wide in amazement.

Then they made a wild scramble for it. They fought among themselves all that afternoon for the money. Some of them got away with little fortunes. Some ran away with their pockets bulging with notes. Others were left with notes that got torn up in the scrambling and fighting. Big John himself was beaten by the others and got nothing. They ran away and left him.

What happened to Big John after that no one knows. Some say he dreamed again of the water woman that night and she took him away in the dream. Some say he went to the koker several nights to look for her but never found her, and so he drowned himself in the river. Others say that the water woman sent her water people for him, and they took him to live with her in her home at the bottom of the river.

But if you go down to the koker near Parika on any night of the full moon, you will see the water woman sitting with her back to the road and her face to the river, combing her long, black, shiny hair in the moonlight. You will also see a tall, big man with broad shoulders standing close beside her.

The Gloves

GARNETT RADCLIFFE

I hadn't gone into Mr Robinson's shop to buy gloves. I had gone in hoping to find among the miscellany of junk that filled the place literally from floor to ceiling a bracket for a shaving cabinet, and I was poking about when the gloves caught my eye. They were on a chair near the door, and I did not at once realize that they were for sale.

'One of your customers has left his gloves behind,' I told Mr Robinson. 'You'd better put them somewhere safe for he may come back for them.'

Mr Robinson, who is middle-aged and worried looking, clicked his tongue—a sign of annoyance.

'I'd have sworn I put 'em away,' he said. 'Gettin' absent-minded in my old age, that's what I am. No, they haven't been left behind. I gave that ferrety-faced loafer Joe Larkin ten bob for them the other day. 'Spect he pinched 'em, but that's not my business . . . You feel the quality . . . Real hogskin, those gloves are.'

I examined them. They were genuine hogskin with a wool lining, and they had been very little worn.

'How much?' I asked.

'Twelve and six to you,' Mr Robinson said. 'They're a bargain. Last you a lifetime those will!'

As it happened I needed a pair of gloves, having left my own much inferior ones on a bus a few days before. When I'd tried them on and found they fitted perfectly the chance of obtaining a first-class article at a very moderate price overcame my dislike of second-hand goods.

'Twelve and six it is,' I said.

When I'd returned to the bachelor flat I was renting in that beehive called Harbinger Mansions I examined my purchase again. Yes, they were excellent gloves and practically unsoiled except just inside each wrist where both wool linings had a ring of faint, brownish stains. I told myself no one would ever notice that and put them away in the top left-hand drawer of my chest of drawers.

I don't keep a diary, nor have I a very retentive memory. When I say it was about a week later that the first incident in connection with those gloves occurred, I am merely hazarding a guess.

It was such a trivial incident that at the time it hardly registered itself on my mind. It was only when subsequent happenings induced me to look back that I recalled it as being the first of a chain of rather curious events.

All that happened was that the gloves seemed to have moved themselves inside the drawer. When I went to take them out— it was a cold, wet morning most appropriate for the wearing of wool-lined, hogskin gloves—they were not stretched on a collar-box as I distinctly remembered having left them. They were on top of some socks in the front portion of the drawer, and the fingers were curled into the palms so that they looked like a pair of clenched fists.

Of course there was an obvious explanation. Mrs Hubbard, the amiable lady who 'did out' my flat during my absence must have been doing a bit of prying. She'd noticed the gloves, had taken them out to try them on her own fat hands, and had omitted to replace them as she'd found them.

I decided I'd say nothing to Mrs Hubbard. She was a good old soul whose services I wouldn't have risked losing for half-a-dozen pairs of gloves.

I wore the gloves that day with satisfaction. They were warm and comfortable and they looked good. A gentleman's gloves, I flattered myself. Gloves are great conveyors of personality, and I could picture their previous owner—their real owner I mean, not the ferrety-faced Mr Larkin who had sold them to Mr Robinson—as having been the old-fashioned country squire type who appreciated good leather, sound horses and vintage port. It may seem ridiculous to deduce all that from a pair of gloves, but when I looked at these with their hallmark of quality and faint indentations on the palms as if they had once gripped reins, that was the very vivid impression I got.

When I got back that night they were too wet to be replaced in the drawer, so I put them on the back of a chair within reasonable distance of the radiator.

And so came incident No.2, which can be just as easily explained away as the first. Presumably, I hadn't balanced them very well on the chair, or they were disturbed by a draught, for in the morning I found they had fallen to the floor and rolled several feet away from the chair towards the window. Somehow when I saw them lying on the carpet, backs uppermost and fingers spread out and slightly curved, I was put in mind of a man crawling on his face.

The impression was so strong I disliked picking them up. They still felt a little damp and—presumably because of the radiator—warm as if they had recently been worn.

After that there was a spell of fine weather during which I had no occasion to wear or to think of gloves. I'd quite forgotten them when one evening when I was asking for my letters the hall porter gave me a message.

'Mrs Hubbard, the lady who does your flat, thinks you've got mice, sir,' he said. 'If you've no objection I'll arrange for a trap to be left in the bedroom.'

Mice are not to be tolerated in a hive for humans such as Harbinger Mansions. I told the porter I thought a trap would be an excellent idea. That evening it was the first thing I saw when I entered my bedroom. Probably on the advice of Mrs Hubbard it had been placed close to the chest of drawers.

That night I heard the mice myself. From the sounds they made they were robust mice. Lying awake and furious, I could picture a couple of large rats romping about inside the chest of drawers. A rat hunt in pyjamas and bare feet didn't appeal to me, so I pulled the sheets round my head and eventually, despite the scrabbling, scratching sounds, I fell asleep.

Next morning the trap was empty. I looked in the chest of drawers. Only the top left-hand drawer had been disturbed. In there the rats had worked havoc. Handkerchiefs, socks and collars had been flung about and mixed as if by a rake, and the paper which lined the bottom of the drawer had been scraped up and torn. I found the gloves almost hidden beneath the paper. I put the drawer to rights and went out cursing all rats.

The following night was very similar, except that the rats were even more frisky. After listening to the scrabbling, bumping sounds for a couple of hours, I sprang out of bed in desperation and yanked open the drawer whence the sounds seemed to come.

The contents had been disturbed and flung about, but no sign of a rat. I returned to bed leaving the drawer open. I must have scared the rats for silence followed. As I was dropping off to sleep I thought I heard a soft flop, flop, as if the intruders had hopped from the drawer on the carpet, but I was too weary to get up again.

'Git, you brutes!' I hissed, and I turned deeper into the pillow.

I didn't sleep as well that night as I usually do. Several times I half woke to hear the rats scampering about the room, and once I'd an unpleasant nightmare in which a pair of soft, flabby hands seemed to be groping round my face and neck. My last recollection is of a sound of drumming at the window as if someone were tapping on the glass with his fingers.

In the morning I found the rats had pulled the gloves out of the drawer. After a search I found them beneath the chest of drawers whence I had to retrieve them with the crook of my umbrella. They were dusty and crumpled, so that they looked like a couple of dead crabs. Somehow I disliked handling them.

I wasn't going to suffer another such night. After I'd put my drawer straight I went down and spoke my mind to the hall porter. If he could not get rid of the rats, I threatened I would leave Harbinger Mansions.

He promised strong measures. In the evening I found a second trap had been installed and poisoned bait had been left in strategic points. Hoping for the best I went to bed early.

I slept badly and had a dream in which I saw a finger beckoning to me from the top of the chest of drawers. Then I dropped off only to be woken a little later by the sound of my door opening as if someone had given it a violent jerk. I sat up. Sure enough the door opening on the corridor was open. I could see the dim blue light which always burns in the corridor and I could feel a cold draught.

Cursing and rather scared I got out of bed, trying to assure myself I hadn't closed the door firmly and the draught had blown it open. As I was about to close it I heard a frightened yell from the direction of the main stairway.

I hurried down the dim corridor fearful of seeing I knew not what. On the landing a figure cowered against the wall. It was one of the night-porters, an elderly individual with a bibulous countenance and a ragged white moustache. As he pointed down the stairs his hand shook, and his face was ashen.

'Spiders!' he gasped. 'A couple of whopping great brown spiders! Gawd, am I seein' things?'

I told him that what he'd imagined to be spiders were in all probability the rats that had been haunting my bedroom. After a bit I persuaded him to accompany me down the main stairway to the entrance hall where we turned on lights and peered under chairs and sofas. There were no rats to be seen. I told the porter that what Harbinger Mansions needed was a good fox-terrier.

'They *were* spiders,' he insisted. 'Rats don't run like this,' and he illustrated what he meant by making his hands dart along the counter at the enquiry desk, the fingers moving very quickly so that they looked like the legs of running spiders. I wish he hadn't done that, for later on I had yet another creepy dream in which I was following a pair of hands that scuttled like crabs along wet streets and roads until they reached a dirty little house with no lights where they groped up the wall and vanished through a broken window into a dark room. I seemed to hear then a scream like the hoot of a railway engine and I woke up sweating and trembling.

But at least the rats had left my room, never to return again. Apparently they'd either eaten the gloves or dragged them off with them for nesting purposes, for although I searched high and low they were nowhere to be found.

And is that the end of the story? Well, on that point I'd rather not offer an opinion. But I will relate something that some readers may think casts a light on what happened in my flat.

The facts came to me through the mouth of Mr Robinson. I was poking about in his shop after my wont when he asked me if I still had the gloves I'd bought.

'They've vanished,' I said, which was nearer the truth than if I'd just said I'd lost them.

'Vanished, eh?' said Mr Robinson. 'Well, the fellow who sold them to me, that ferrety wastrel Joe Larkin, has vanished too! Leastways, he's dead. He's been found strangled in his bed in that old condemned house of his by the Minchley railway line.'

'*Strangled?*' I repeated.

'Yes, strangled,' said Mr Robinson. 'And the police haven't a clue who did it. The murderer wore gloves and he didn't leave a trace. What beats the police is how he got into the house with all the doors and windows fastened. They say he didn't leave so much as a footprint in the dust . . . Anyway Joe Larkin was no loss . . . Do you know where I believe he got the gloves I sold you?'

'Where?' I asked.

'You remember the crash on the Minchley line when the London express collided with a goods train? It happened in the cutting just below Joe's house. He was there all right, but I bet he didn't waste time helping people out of the wreckage. Loot—that would be Joe's game . . .

'I could just see him creeping round the burning coaches like the human rat he was . . . He'd have pinched the wallet off a dying man . . . or the shoes off a dead baby! I bet that's where he found those gloves.'

That was what Mr Robinson told me. Later, curiosity caused me to go to a public library where I could read the back numbers of the papers reporting the Minchley crash. Among the list of the killed I remarked the name of a certain Colonel

Belcher-Price, an ex-Hussar and MFH of the Minchley Hunt. It stated in the paper that he'd had both hands severed at the wrist when his first-class carriage was telescoped by a goods truck.

I'll leave the reader to draw his or her own conclusions . . .

Do You Dance?

LAURENCE STAIG

Was it his imagination? He wasn't sure. There was a soft, fragile music, which seemed to be carried on the breeze. After several days of wandering and climbing in this part of the country, he was beginning to feel that his surroundings were playing tricks on him. The sun appeared fiercer than he had ever seen before, and as the rays bled into the clouds they stained the sky like a wound. The stark, bold outlines of the rocks shimmered in the light, as if they were living things waiting to crawl across the landscape. This was a strange land, almost the dark side of the moon. The lush green wand of Ireland had missed this place.

He shivered, but it was not from any coldness.

There they were again; pipes or whistles, he could not decide which, but the music was wound within the breeze. He stopped and listened again.

'Come on, you!' a cry came from ahead.

Sarah and Heather had gone on, their back-packs, ropes, and tools bobbed like dark blots against the sparse greyness of the rocks and gorse.

'I'm coming,' replied Robert. 'Hang on.'

The girls stopped, waiting for him to catch up.

After several minutes he arrived, breathless. Heather had already opened the map and was peering into the distance, checking her co-ordinates. Sarah's face still seemed to mock him, her mouth upturned at the edges as though she was in possession of a secret which she would never tell. Her dark fringe blew in front of her face. Through her hair, her eyes sparkled. Sarah irritated him; he had never wanted her to join them, but she was Heather's friend and wanted the experience.

Heather smiled at him, her smile warm and sincere.

'Not far now. Holihook should be just over that peak. See the stream down there?' She pointed in the distance.

He nodded and followed her finger.

'That's the Holiwell. It goes through the village. See, look at the map.'

'He can't read maps,' laughed Sarah. 'That's why he belongs to a climbing club. No problem simply going up the side of a mountain.'

'Take a run and jump,' said Robert.

'Stop it, you two,' said Heather with a sigh. 'Come on, we'll soon be there.'

She folded up the map and put it into the pocket of her yellow parka. She squeezed his arm, and smiled at him with her eyes. How he wished it were just the two of them. Usually it was such fun with just the two of them, the wind in their hair. The breeze blew up again. This time a soft whistle echoed round the hillside.

'What about that music?' said Robert.

The two girls looked at him. Heather frowned. 'What music?'

'Listen,' said Robert as he stood quite, quite still. The wind dropped and there was a silence once more.

'I thought I heard pipes, or maybe it was a tin whistle. I heard it earlier. I thought you did as well and just hadn't said anything.'

Sarah pulled a face and went ahead. Heather pushed her long blonde hair around her ears and cocked her head to one side.

'I think I can hear it,' she said, after a moment. 'Isn't it coming from over there?' She nodded in the direction they were heading.

'You're imagining things,' called Sarah over her shoulder.

'It's a bit of a dump really,' said Sarah, as she bounced on the corner of the bed. 'I'll take this one.'

Robert hung his jacket on the back of the door, and glanced down at the metal cot bed beneath the window.

'I suppose this will have to be mine,' he mumbled.

'I'll have that if you like,' said Heather. 'I really don't mind. I can sleep on a tree branch if necessary.'

'No,' Robert glanced up, suddenly. 'It's all right. I'm happy in this thing; you can have the other bed.' He turned to Sarah. 'Look, I got us a good deal with the old girl downstairs, so don't blow it. We may all have to share the same room but it's a good size. You know we have to be careful with our money if it's going to last the holiday.'

'Some holiday,' said Sarah. 'Back-packing and climbing in the wildest part of Ireland. All we seem to have done is walk.'

Suddenly there was a gentle knock on the door. It was so unexpected that the three of them fell silent and stared at one another blankly. Slowly, the door was opened and a small woman dressed in black, her hair tied into a bun, stepped into the room.

'Oh, I'm sorry,' she said. 'I thought perhaps you'd all taken a stroll. Welcome. Here now, nobody's been in this room in a long time. Few travellers visit the inn, especially at this time. Here, let me open the windows for you—air the place, blow away the old cobwebs, eh? That's the thing.'

The woman opened a pair of paint-blistered frames. The inn overlooked the village square. Outside, the hum of passing people floated up to them. She tucked in the corners of the two proper beds, and then turned down the sheets.

'On a walking holiday, you say?' she said to nobody in particular. 'I think it's good to see young people take the air and to be able to share like this. That's a grand thing. It's so good to have you here at a time like this.'

Robert was about to reply when another sound, something oddly familiar, drifted past the window. It was the pipes he had heard earlier, but this time they sounded more distinct, sharper and nearer too, and this time they all heard them.

'What are they?' he asked.

The woman ignored his question. Instead, she took some towels out of a cupboard and folded them across a rail beside the small porcelain sink.

'Those pipes, or flutes, what are they, please?' said Robert again.

'Oh, the pipes?' she laughed. 'Pay them no mind. It's a little custom we have, and you've arrived on the eve.'

'Who's playing them?' Sarah asked, as she started to unpack.

'And where?' said Heather. 'They sound as though they're everywhere.'

The woman smiled and shook out one of the towels. 'Oh, they're played here and there, mostly by the older women of the town. It's a custom, like I said. Sometimes they go up on the northern hillside and sit and play. It's been going on all week. It stops after tonight.' For a moment she stood in silence and watched the three of them. It was as if she were waiting. She coughed. 'Say, young lady—do you need anything washing?'

Sarah had pulled a dirty shirt from her bag. On the back was the outline of a goat. Robert had given one to each of them.

'There's no need,' she began.

The woman took the shirt and started to sing to herself, something Irish and folksy. Suddenly, she froze and glanced at Sarah. She was unsmiling. 'You're a pretty young thing! Do you dance?'

Sarah tried to warm to the woman, but for some reason a cold sliver of unreasoned fear crept beneath her skin.

'Yes, yes, I do actually,' said Sarah stiffly.

'Good, good,' said the woman with a smile. 'It's a fine thing to dance. We end up with a right old time. They've been making the music for her, it's all for her. She'll be there.'

Robert tipped his bag on to the bed. A similar shirt to Sarah's fell out. The woman saw it.

'My, oh my,' said the woman. 'There's another. I'll have me a collection. It's a pretty thing, here.'

'It's our climbing club symbol,' said Sarah.

Before he could say anything, the woman had grabbed the shirt and held it with the other.

'I bet you have one too?' She held Heather with a gaze of stone. Heather swallowed.

'No,' she said.

'You have so,' said Sarah sharply.

Heather gripped her bag. She did not know why, but she didn't want to give her shirt to this woman.

The woman glared.

'You can wash mine, by all means,' said Robert with a snort.

All of a sudden a surly red-faced man with mutton-chop whiskers and a white apron appeared at the door. His eyes were harder than stone and for a moment he glared at the woman.

'You're wanted downstairs, mother,' he said. 'The little one's crying for you. I'm sure these folks can manage.'

The three of them walked through the village, and they walked together. Over the past week they had separated amongst the hills, each climbing a favourite peak and calling to the others, but not here, not in the village high street.

'Is it me,' said Heather, 'or are they watching us?'

Robert said nothing. Sarah remained tight-lipped too. Their mid-afternoon stroll had turned into something slightly less pleasant. Nobody was aggressive, but nobody seemed friendly either. People stood in doorways and watched in silence as they passed. Sometimes a conversation would stop mid-sentence, and an eyebrow would rise. Robert nodded politely.

'Have you noticed?' asked Heather.

'Noticed what?' Robert replied.

'It's busy. Strangely it's very busy. And look at some of the locals, they seem so old.'

Robert hadn't noticed this before, but she was right. There were a lot of older-looking people around, many standing on corners, simply standing and staring.

'Over there,' whispered Sarah, nodding in the direction of a courtyard. 'Look at those women.'

Robert and Heather followed her gaze. Beside another inn was an open courtyard. Washing lines were strung across the yard and half a dozen women or more were hanging out clothes.

'Must be laundry day,' said Robert.

'No, no, it's not right,' said Heather. 'I can't place it exactly.'

They stopped walking. 'I mean,' continued Heather, 'there's stacks of clothes, piles of them. Look at those baskets.' Further lines of women were gathering in the square now, and were hanging out shirts, trousers and skirts.

As they walked on, Robert glanced down a narrow side turning. Washing lines had been run from the upper storeys of the houses, above the street. Women were busy hanging clothes on these lines, which were already sagging from the weight.

'Perhaps it's just a clean village. That old girl was keen to get her hands on our shirts,' said Sarah as she popped a piece of gum into her mouth. 'Perhaps they all have dirty jobs.' She almost laughed, but Heather did not.

All of a sudden, the pipes started up again. A low wind blew through the village street; people almost stepped to one side to allow it through. But intertwined with the tuneless melody was a voice. There was no doubt this time: a cry, almost a wail. The people around them stopped and glanced upwards, as if expecting something more. The voice died with the wind as the sounds of the pipes grew louder.

Then Robert noticed the women. Several crossed themselves, and some kissed crucifixes which they wore around their necks.

Heather tugged at Robert's sleeve. He glanced down at her and put a finger to his lips. The level of the music lowered; unmistakably this time it came from the surrounding hills.

'I think I'd like to go back to the inn,' said Heather. Sarah gazed beyond the hillside.

As they walked back to the inn, the pipes cried out above the village. They sounded like strange birds, competing somehow with themselves. Now there seemed more of them. No longer a barely pretty tune, trills clashed against lower notes and there seemed to be no escape from the growing cacophony. Somewhere within, once again a voice was struggling to be heard.

Even Sarah seemed nervous and was uncharacteristically silent. As the three of them turned the corner which led to the inn, they passed a small track road to the left. Here, more women carried baskets of washing; and almost with urgency, more washing lines were being stretched across the road. But what stopped Robert in his tracks was the view beyond. The

road led through to a gorse patch which led up the hillside.
Sitting beside a rock, a little way up, was what seemed to be an
old woman. She was bent almost double, and was dressed in a
long sackcloth robe like a monk's. It was impossible to see her

face, which was hidden in a hood, but bunches of her hair, wild and long, stretched down in front of her. Her hair was the darkest, deepest red. Bony fingers were close to her face, as though she were calling. Behind her, the sun was setting. The rays bled through the strands of wispy cloud like veins.

For some reason, Robert whispered, 'My God.'

He looked away for a second, and when he looked back she was gone.

'Visitors, travellers?' said a voice from out of nowhere.

Heather spun round. In the shadows of a doorway stood a grey-bearded figure. It was a man, who sucked on a hooked pipe. One eye was half closed.

'Travellers, I said?'

'Yes,' replied Heather. 'Yes, that's right.'

He grinned. Then he added, 'Do you dance?'

Sarah laughed. The music of the pipes crept from the hills again.

'Come on, girl, answer me question, do you dance?'

She grinned and twirled for him.

This time Heather did not reply. Robert hurried them on. Something glinted in Sarah's eye. For some reason, the music had begun to appeal.

The pipes continued into nightfall. Sarah tossed and tied herself up into her sheets. Heather lay awake staring at the ceiling, saying nothing, but her fingers made a claw and dug into the bed clothes. Robert felt strangely drowsy. There were occasions when the whistling melody melted into a cry, and it grew and ascended as though it were a bird climbing and climbing into the darker, more secret parts of the sky. It was hypnotic.

Heather got up and walked to the rear window. It looked out into the courtyard. The woman who had shown them to their room was joined by others. She was laying out two white shirts on a bush. But then, another villager lifted a small bucket containing a dark liquid which reflected the moonlight, and poured it on to the shirts. Heather narrowed her eyes; she wondered what was going on. But then she saw what had filled the bucket. Nearby, two black cocks lay on a wooden table beside what looked like a butcher's chopper. She caught her breath and looked away.

'What . . . what are they doing?' she whispered.

The sound of the pipes grew.

'I can't stand it, why don't they shut up!' yelled Sarah suddenly. She sat up and put her face in her hands.

Within moments she had bounded out of bed and crossed the room.

'Where, where are you going?' asked Heather.

'Out. The bathroom. I don't know, I just need to get up, move around.' With that, she left the room, closing the door behind her.

'I'll see that she's all right,' said Heather.

The music of the pipes floated into Robert's head, but now the cries were more insistent. Perhaps there was really no music, only cries. Time passed. He was knocked from his semi-dream by a scratching noise. It was quite distinct, like nails on a board. It repeated itself, a straight, precise grating.

For a moment he wondered if there was a mouse, or worse still perhaps a rat, in the room. Shapes appeared to flicker on the ceiling. Was there something going on outside?

He looked across to the floor. The silvery beams of the moon threw a dark huddled shadow on to the polished bedroom boards. He instinctively looked up at the window above him. There was something pressed against the glass. It was only after a moment that he realized it was a face. It was huge and fierce, a woman's face with folded creases of flesh within which were eyes that shone with a white marble blankness. Her blood-red hair billowed behind her as though she might be floating there, in space. Her mouth was a dark cavern, and her tongue lolled like a bloated worm. A hand of thin spindly fingers scratched down the glass. But it was her cry that drowned out everything else. It was the cry he thought he had heard before, that mingled with the pipes; but this time it was a wail, alone, a pure scream from the bottom of an abyss.

Robert sat upright with a shudder which shook his bones. A coldness he had never felt before rippled through his flesh.

The pipes were everywhere. Outside, in the street below, came the sounds of people. There were cries, whoops of joy, screams. He rolled out of his cot and looked back at the window. There was nobody there. Hesitating at first, he moved forward to peer out. Had he been dreaming, he wondered? But the scene below now occupied his thoughts. There were crowds of them, villagers. They were a mixture of young and old, but the staggering ungainly gait showed him that most of the figures were elderly—almost ancient. And they were dancing. They made a grotesque line, weaving and swaying. There was something about the way they moved which bothered him deeply. The faces glowed with a gleam of madness.

Then he saw Heather.

She was in the centre of a ring of villagers which had formed close by the line of dancers. She was screaming, her hands holding the sides of her face as though she was grappling with the wind. The bouncing chain of people held something like rags above their heads, waving them as if they were grotesque banners. The light of the moon glistened on the whiteness of the rags. There were marks, streaks of something wet which glistened beneath the silvery rays of the moon. He swallowed hard as he realized what it was: an awful brownish red wash of colour. A blonde-haired girl, daubed with the same wash, led the chain. The laugh was unmistakable. It was Sarah.

Robert rushed out of the room. In the tap room downstairs, villagers were heaving their bones to the music of the pipes, stepping to the terrible music. They seemed not to see him as he pushed past them. It was not until he stood in the doorway that all became clearer. Twisting and turning within the dancers, like a flickering shadow, was a red-haired woman. She held pieces of rags above her head—almost in triumph. It was the face at the window.

He staggered back. Droplets, like generous beads of sweat, dripped from the dancers to the floor to make pools of blood. It was almost a dance of death. Then he saw the woman from the inn. Triumphantly she swept into the dancers and carried a shirt; it was another similar to the one the red-haired woman had held in her claws, but this time there was something about the garment which identified it: an image on the back—*like the outline of a goat*. She looked at him for seconds only. She gave it to the red-haired woman who tore at it with glee. With a groan he realized who the shirts had belonged to.

He cried and rushed forward, grabbing Sarah by the hand. She was somewhere else, in a grim place of reverie, and her mouth was wild and open. He yanked her behind him as he forced his way through the ring, and caught Heather by the waist.

With tears in his eyes, he ran and ran and ran from that place, the two girls beside him. He ran until the sounds of the pipes, the cries, and the screams could be heard no longer. Together they walked to the next village and arrived at sunrise, in silence.

Later the next day, as they waited for the ferry, Robert was told the story. He heard it from an old boy—a man of the road—in exchange for a few coins. He said they should never have been in Holihook that night. For Holihook had long been a community in the grip of a Banshee, who once a year foretold the deaths that were due to the families there. Usually, the Banshee would wash the clothes of those about to die, and hang them out to dry. But the villagers now filled all of the washing lines themselves with their own washing, denying the Banshee. To appease the Banshee, they would prepare for the dance, and the music that would drown out her voice. Nobody would die that year if nobody heard her summoning cries, and if she was unable to wash their clothes.

But sometimes, just sometimes, the old man had said, they would let her have items of travellers' clothing if any visited their village. They would ritually bury the clothes in the earth, and wash them by moonlight in the blood of two black cocks. This would transfer the foretold deaths to the unwary travellers. Then he had laughed. 'It's only a story,' he said.

The three of them never spoke of the events.

Something had happened that had placed distance between them. Heather became quieter still and rarely climbed, and Robert was easily startled by the innocent flap of washing on a windy day. But Sarah continued to bear that smile, as though now she had her secret.

It was not until much later that year whilst climbing with their club on a challenging rock face, that Robert remembered and realized. He had heard the cry of the thing at the window, and the Banshee had handled and torn at their shirts.

The accident was horrific. As Sarah and Robert plunged off the mountain face, grotesquely clawing and dancing in the wind as they fell, he heard the pipes once again.

The Junk Room

TERRY TAPP

On the outskirts of a tiny Devonshire village, surrounded by a wall of Dartmoor granite, a grey,
forbidding house looks out over the rolling hills. Ivy
trails over the blistered paint of a board which once offered the
house for sale, and a couple of rusted iron gates hang crazily
from granite pillars, groaning against the wind, crashing against
the wall like cymbals.

Curving away from the frenzied, captive gates, the drive
sweeps up towards Graston House, circling a raised bed of
brambles and weeds. The drive is lined with cherry trees,
regimentally spaced, yet bowed by the sharp winds of the moor.
The studded door is locked and boarded now; the small-paned
windows sightless with the growth of dust.

Inside the house time is frozen. Food has rotted in the
refrigerator; clothes hang on wooden pegs in the hall. And, in

the bedrooms, the sheets and blankets lie in disarray upon the beds, thrown aside carelessly—and left.

It is ten years since I put the "For Sale" sign in front of Graston House, and I have no hopes now of ever selling it again. Indeed, I shall do everything in my power to dissuade people from buying it—unlikely conduct for an estate agent, I admit, but I have good reason.

Although I have not set foot inside the house since I sold it to the Carter family, I know that the roof is in a bad state of repair and that the rain has penetrated. Left unrepaired, it is only a matter of time before the house will decay.

The story you are about to read has been assembled from the conversation I had with Mrs Carter, the present owner of Graston House, and the many letters she wrote to me. These are the facts of the matter, supported by my own personal knowledge, Mrs Carter's accounts, and other reliable sources. So many stories are currently circulating about Graston House (stories of a light moving from window to window and of dreadful screamings and strange happenings) that I felt it my duty to set the record straight.

I well remember the look of surprise on Tom Carter's face when I immediately accepted his offer to buy the house. 'But aren't you going to check with the owners?' he asked.

'No need,' I assured him. 'The owners have given me permission to accept the first reasonable offer for Graston House, and yours is not an unreasonable offer, Mr Carter.'

The roof, being the most expensive item to repair, was patched temporarily whilst the Carter family set to work modernizing the inside of Graston House. It took two years of hard work to rewire the place and install central heating, decorate the rooms and tile the kitchen. Ancient lead plumbing was replaced with copper pipes; green-painted walls were hung with bright, fresh wallpaper; and the blackened varnish which smothered the doors was burnt away, to be replaced with glistening white gloss paint. Now there was only one room left to decorate.

Tom Carter and his wife, Alice, had used this room to store furniture and toys, books, suitcases and decorating materials. Quite justifiably it had earned its name—the Junk Room.

Now that the end of the decorating was in sight, the Carter

family set to work with renewed enthusiasm. Robin (a year older than his brother, Jason) worked with paint-brush and water, soaking the paper so that it would be easier to scrape from the walls. Their father tackled the paintwork with a roaring blowlamp, filling the air with the scent of burnt paint and wood. As they worked, the two boys chatted excitably above the roar of the blowlamp, tackling the heavy wallpaper with vigour. Within the space of two hours, three of the walls were stripped clean, but the fourth, above the green marble fireplace, proved stubborn.

Mr Carter noticed a square-shaped bump under the wallpaper and advised the boys not to go near it with their scrapers. 'It could be a gaslight outlet or, perhaps, an old electric socket,' he said. 'As soon as I've finished burning the paint off the door, I'll have a look at it.'

Later, armed with a screwdriver, Tom Carter gently levered away the layers of paper to expose a thin block of wood which had been screwed to the wall. The screws were rusty, but they eventually yielded to his largest screwdriver. Taking great care, Mr Carter levered the wooden block from the wall.

There were no wires or pipes behind the block, and the plaster (apart from the four screwholes) was intact. Tom Carter stared at the wall.

'What is it, Dad?' Jason asked, noticing the strange manner in which his father was regarding the wall. 'What have you found?'

Robin paused from collecting up some of the wallpaper and glanced across the room at the two of them, a puzzled expression on his face. 'What are you looking at?' he asked. 'Come and help me with this paper.'

When they did not reply, he went over to see what had taken their attention.

Painted on the wall, a few inches above the mantel-shelf of the fireplace, were two eyes, one slightly larger than the other.

The eyes glistened, fresh and dewy, as if they had been painted only seconds before. Surrounded by cream paint, they stared out from the wall, disembodied, complete in every detail. Rimmed with long black lashes, the blood-crazed whites of the eyes contrasted vividly with the bright blue irises. The pupils of the eyes were jet black, dilated and bright.

'They look so real,' breathed Jason, his hand reaching out to touch the paintwork. 'I wonder why someone took the trouble to paint them?' Suddenly, as if shocked by an invisible electric force, he withdrew his hand and looked away from the wall. 'I don't like them, Dad. They're evil.'

Tom Carter laughed at that. 'How can you tell? You need more than just a pair of eyes to come to that conclusion.'

'They do look real,' Robin agreed. 'If you walk around the room, the eyes seem to be following.'

'An optical illusion,' Mr Carter said. 'It's all in the mind.'

'Cover it over, Dad,' Jason said, his eyes still averted from the penetrating gaze of the painted eyes. 'Please—'

'Now don't be silly, Jason.' A tone of impatience had crept into Tom Carter's voice. He was annoyed at his own reaction to the eyes and felt the need to dismiss the matter.

After lunch, when Mrs Carter had seen the paintings, she agreed with Jason. 'I don't like them,' she said, turning away. 'Someone must have had a sick sense of humour to paint them on the wall.'

'But why did someone take the trouble to screw a wooden block over them?' Robin asked. 'Surely they could have scraped the wall, or simply papered over the eyes without going to all that trouble?'

'Which is precisely what we are going to do,' said his father cheerfully. 'I'll burn the paint off the wall before we paper.' He knelt down and turned the tap on the gas blowlamp, holding a lighted match near the outlet. Nothing happened. Puzzled, he shook the blowlamp against his ear. 'Funny—' he mumbled. 'Plenty of gas in it. The jet must be blocked up.' Using the thin wire pricker he worked at the fine, pinprick jet, scraping away the film deposit. 'There—that should do it.' He turned the tap and smiled as the blowlamp gave out a healthy hissing sound. 'Now, where are the matches? I had them a minute ago.' He turned off the tap and looked around the room.

The search for the matches was interrupted by a loud knocking at the front door. 'I expect that's the garden fertilizer I ordered yesterday,' Mr Carter said. 'Will you show them where to unload it, Robin?' Unable to find the matches, he put the blowlamp down by the door and followed the boys downstairs.

The unloading and stacking of the heavy sacks took quite a while, and when they had finished they decided to stop work for the day. After dinner Tom Carter wanted to spread some of the fertilizer on the garden, and Robin volunteered to help. Jason, protesting loudly, was sent to have a shower.

And that is when the first 'accident' occurred.

As Jason started to undress, he heard a soft, swishing sound immediately behind him. Alarmed, he spun around. There was no one there, but he noticed the handle of the bathroom door slowly turning. A gentle clicking sounded from the lock, and Jason noticed that the key was missing. 'Robin!' he cried. 'Stop playing about!'

He waited, listening, blood pounding in his ears.

'Robin! You know I don't like being locked in!'

No reply.

Jason tried the door handle, rattled it, then shouted at the top of his voice. 'If you don't let me out of here I'll kick the door down!'

A low, rumbling noise came from the landing; soft, filled with malice. Jason felt a cold draught of air around his shoulders. 'Let me out! Let me out!'

Suddenly the lock gave out a sharp report, and the handle turned. Slowly, slowly the door opened, and Jason found himself staring into the eyes of his mother. 'What on earth are you doing?' she demanded crossly.

'Robin locked me in!' Jason cried. 'You wait—I'll get him for this!'

'He did not lock you in,' said Mrs Carter. 'Robin has been in the garden, with your father.'

'Well, someone locked me in,' Jason said. He looked up at his mother. 'Was it you?'

Mrs Carter removed the key from the lock and replaced it on the inside of the door, her hand trembling slightly. 'No,' she said. 'I didn't do it, Jason. Now hurry up and take your shower. Dad and Robin will be wanting to use it later.' She turned away before Jason could see the worried expression on her face.

Later, after he had showered and changed into his night-clothes, Jason ran downstairs into the warm kitchen. Mrs Carter was applying glue to a broken vase. 'I still think Robin locked me in,' he told her.

'And I think you're pulling my leg,' she said, not looking up from her task. 'You must have removed the key from the door, otherwise how could you possibly get locked in when the key is always kept on the inside?'

Deciding to leave the incident for the time being, Jason went over to the vase. 'What happened?' he asked. He knew that the vase was very expensive and that it had been a present from his father. 'Does Dad know you've broken it?'

'I didn't break it,' said his mother. 'We heard a noise in the kitchen, and when we came in the vase was on the floor.' She glanced up at the wall cabinet upon which the vase had rested for almost two years. 'I can't understand why it fell.'

Jason looked out of the kitchen window and noted that Robin was forking dead leaves on to a smouldering bonfire. 'Are you sure he didn't sneak indoors and lock me in the bathroom?' he asked.

'Positive,' came the reply. 'He's been out there with your father since before you went to get ready for bed.' Mrs Carter checked her watch and tapped the glass with her forefinger significantly. 'Which reminds me, young Jason. Time for you to go to bed.'

'May I have a read first?' Jason asked.

'Ten minutes,' agreed Mrs Carter.

'Twenty,' Jason countered, knowing that a compromise would be reached at fifteen.

'All right,' Mrs Carter said absently.

'Thanks, Mum!' Jason, surprised by the ease of his victory, dashed from the kitchen to take full advantage of the twenty minutes' reading time. Such was his haste that he pulled the kitchen door harder than he normally would have, and the sound of splintering glass stopped him in his tracks. He turned, then opened the door. 'Sorry, Mum—' he started to say.

Mrs Carter was standing in front of the back door, which led into the garden. The eight small panes of glass in the door were broken, shards of glass lying on the kitchen tiles, glistening like frost.

'It wasn't your fault, Jason,' she said, her voice taut and strained. She spoke again, firmly this time. 'Please go to bed.'

Hearing the tone of her voice, Jason did as he was told, carefully closing the door behind him.

Mrs Carter called out to her husband. 'Tom, will you come in here for a minute?'

Leaving Robin to pile more leaves on the bonfire, Mr Carter hurried across the garden. As he approached the kitchen door, he shouted: 'What is it? Are you hurt?'

'No,' said Mrs Carter. 'Just come into the kitchen. I want to talk to you.'

'How did this happen?' her husband asked as he stepped over the broken glass.

Mrs Carter stared at him awhile before taking breath to reply. 'You'll think I'm being silly—' she began.

He sat down at the kitchen table. 'What's the matter?'

'Things seem to be happening,' she said.

'Things?'

'First the vase—' She laughed, nervously, as if afraid to continue.

Tom Carter gave a grim smile. 'These things come in threes,' he said.

'I was going to show you this later, when the boys were in bed,' she replied, opening the pantry door and reaching inside. She closed the door and turned to face him, revealing what it was she held in her hand.

'What is it?' he asked.

'What *was* it?' she said. 'It *was* our electric kettle.'

He took the twisted, crumpled metal from her. What had once been a shining copper kettle was now almost beyond recognition, screwed up like tinfoil, pressed tight and flat. 'Good God,' Mr Carter said as he examined it. 'What on earth happened?'

'I don't know,' she said, holding on to the table, her voice cracking as words spilled out. 'Why should a vase just suddenly tumble like that? Why should the back door slam when there isn't a breath of wind?' She glanced at the kettle, then looked quickly away, as if afraid to gaze upon it too long. 'And why . . .'

'How did it happen?'

Mrs Carter looked at her husband fearfully. 'I heard a noise, and when I looked over at the kettle it was folding itself up— it—it was just folding itself up as if a hand had enclosed it, and—'

Mr Carter stared at the kettle, then tried to twist the flattened spout around. 'Heat,' he said. 'You must have switched the kettle on without putting water in it. It's a wonder it didn't blow the fuse.'

'It was not switched on,' she said.

He smiled to comfort her. 'Perhaps the socket is faulty. Heat must have caused this. Look, I can't move it.' He made another attempt to twist the metal.

Mrs Carter nodded slowly. But she was not convinced.

By the time the glass had been swept away and the door had been boarded up to make the house safe and draught-free for the night it was ten o'clock. They decided to go to bed, then, and by eleven o'clock the family were all asleep.

The night was dark, low clouds snuffing out the stars so that the house lay sheathed in a black cloak. Nothing moved; it was as if the creatures of the night were afraid to show themselves. Even the leaves on the black-draped trees were still hanging limp and exhausted from frozen branches. Darkness closed in around the granite walls, stifling the building. And the Carter family slept on . . .

Jason was the first to awake, his heart thudding in his chest. Something had caused him to sit bolt upright in his bed, and he stared into the blackness of his room, confused, unable to collect his senses. Suddenly his bed tilted from under him, and he rolled over, his hands reaching out for something to grasp. He lay where he had fallen, bewildered, too afraid to cry out. And the darkness closed in on him like a cold blanket, suffocating.

Mr and Mrs Carter, hearing the noise, were instantly awake.

'What is it, Tom?' Mrs Carter asked drowsily.

'Thought I heard something,' he replied, cocking his head to one side. 'Maybe it was a car backfiring.'

He was about to lie down when he heard the scream.

Over the years Mr and Mrs Carter had become used to hearing one or the other of their children cry out during the night. But this scream was different. Chilling. It came without warning, wild and piercing, animal-like in its intensity, so that it caused the hairs on Mr Carter's neck to rise up as if a cold hand had brushed against him.

Instantly he threw aside the bedclothes and put his feet upon the carpet. With a cry he withdrew them, his hand fumbling for the switch on the bedside light.

'What is it?' Mrs Carter cried, sensing his alarm.

'Don't know—' The room became bathed in a white, dazzling light for a moment, then the bulb cracked and glass splintered out from the shade, plunging them into a deeper darkness. 'The floor,' he said. 'Something hot on the floor.'

'Hot?'

Jason's next scream brought Mr Carter from the bed immediately. Without thought for his own safety he ran across the room and grasped the door handle, pulling it back hard.

The door was locked.

'Locked!' he cried. 'The door's locked!'

'But it can't be,' said Mrs Carter. 'The lock doesn't work, Tom. Try again.'

He tugged, harder this time, but the door refused to move. Jason was sobbing now and Mr Carter became desperate in his attempts to open the door. 'It must be stuck, somehow,' he grunted, his hands struggling to gain some movement from the door handle. Then he realized that something cold, something slippery, like a snake, was squeezing between his toes. He stepped back, only to find himself deeper in what appeared to be a pool of slime. 'Find a torch!' he cried. 'It's in the bedside cabinet!'

Before his wife could make a movement, Jason screamed again, and she cried out, 'Tom!' in desperation.

Mr Carter stood back from the door and charged at it, his shoulder taking the full impact. The door did not move. Again he charged, catching his shoulder on the edge of the thick ornamental beading around the door panel. He recoiled, bruised and shaken. Switching off the socket, he pulled out the plug of the heavy electric bedside lamp and used it as a hammer, pounding the thinner door panels so that they splintered and cracked.

Robin awoke to hear the chaos—Jason screaming, his mother crying out, hammering and splintering. He reached for the light switch which dangled on a cord above his head, and when he pulled it hard the cord wriggled in his fingers, coiling down around his wrists, hissing and spitting viciously. He shook it off with a yell of terror, and, leaping from the bed, he ran across the room to the door. He was about to touch the handle when the room was suddenly lit by a flame. The door was burning! He touched the handle, but it was too hot to grasp. Feeling his way back to the bed, he reached for the blankets to insulate his hands against the heat and, as his fingers touched the bed, the thin, snaking cord was upon him.

By this time Jason had made his way across the landing towards his parents' bedroom, just in time to see the panels of the door split open under the frantic blows from the table lamp. He had never seen such a look of anger on his father's face, and he stood back as the door splintered like matchwood. Together they ran to Robin's room. This time, the door yielded instantly to Mr Carter's shoulder.

'Dad?' Robin's voice echoed in the darkness. 'Dad—what's happening?' He was near to tears.

Mrs Carter pushed past them into the room, her arms outstretched to comfort Robin. And they stood together, frightened and puzzled.

'This has something to do with those eyes in the junk room,' Jason said. 'I wish we'd never started to strip the paper—'

'Tom? What do you think?' Mrs Carter's voice was almost a whisper.

'I think the boy is right,' came the grim reply.

Suddenly books started to peel off the long shelf above Robin's bed, one by one, pages fluttering, then two by two, more, more, faster and faster, book after book. Ten, twenty, forty. The shelf bowed and twisted as if crushed in an invisible press that was snapping the wood, pulling out the thin steel brackets. Jason screamed.

The overhead light flashed on to reveal their ghastly white faces, then it went out, plunging them into greater darkness than before. A switch turned on the wall and fell to the floor, pulling out a length of fizzing, arcing cable. Water dripped from the ceiling, slowly at first, then faster . . . faster . . .

'Let's get out!' Robin shouted. 'The house is falling apart!'

'Stay where you are!' Tom Carter's voice cut through the darkness. 'Don't panic, now. I think this is all an hallucination. The answer lies with those eyes. I . . . I've got to get rid of them.'

'Tom!' Mrs Carter's voice rang out.

Tom Carter paused. 'Yes?'

'Be careful—' was all she could say.

'I've got to get rid of them,' he repeated. 'Take no notice of what you see, or hear. It isn't really happening at all. This is an hallucination. Remember—this can't possibly be happening. Say it. Say it out loud. Repeat after me—this isn't happening. This isn't happening.'

Mrs Carter started chanting. 'This isn't happening.'

'This isn't happening,' Robin mumbled.

'Louder!' cried Mr Carter. 'Shout it out! Louder!'

He turned, slowly making his way along the landing to the small room, his family following a few paces behind, chanting aloud.

The door was open, and a soft, luminous light flowed out on to the landing. It was cold. Tom Carter stood in the doorway and was about to step into the room when Jason screamed out. 'Dad! Look! The floorboards have gone!'

Tom Carter turned to face them, the green light lending his face a sickly appearance.

'This isn't happening,' he said. 'Whatever force this is— whatever evil is coming from those eyes—this is *not* happening to us. Now say it again.'

Almost reluctantly they repeated his words and watched as he bent to pick up the blowlamp. This time the gas hissed out, and the flame leapt from the fine nozzle. Tom Carter looked across the room at the eyes.

Embedded in the wall, the eyes glared out balefully, the light of the flame reflected in them, so that they appeared to move. Tom Carter looked down at the floor, unable to meet that intense stare.

Between the doorway and the fireplace there was an open pit, the walls of which glowed green. He leaned forward, a grim smile briefly flickering across his face. Then he said: 'The eyes are using these hallucinations to defend themselves.'

'Drop something into the hole, Dad,' said Robin. 'That will tell you if it's real, or not.'

'Whatever I drop will *appear* to fall into the hole,' said Mr Carter. 'No. There's only one way. I must have the courage to challenge!'

A low, menacing chuckle filled the air, and the eyes on the wall appeared to half close as if in ecstacy. Tom Carter took a pace forward, the blowlamp roaring vengeance.

At once there was a loud, anguished scream, and the eyes opened wide.

Tom Carter fell. Down into the pit. Down, his shrieks echoing insanely. Mrs Carter rushed forward, her mouth open in a frozen scream.

Down—down—down.

Falling endlessly.

Falling slowly.

Plunging, in slow, slow motion towards the eyes, which had disappeared from the wall and were now waiting . . .

The rest of the story is well documented. Naturally the police visited Graston House and searched for Tom Carter. Some villagers suspect that Mrs Carter murdered her husband and invented the story; others say that her husband left her. After all, when the police investigated the incident they found the floor of that room intact. There were no light switches broken away from the walls, no smashed doors. There was, however, a pair of eyes, freshly painted, staring down from the wall above the fireplace.

Blind Man's Buff

H. RUSSELL WAKEFIELD

W ell, thank heavens that yokel seemed to know the place,' said Mr Cort to himself. '"First to the right, second to the left, black gates." I hope the oaf in Wendover who sent me six miles out of my way will freeze to death. It's not often like this in England—cold as the penny in a dead man's eye.' He'd barely reach the place before dusk. He let the car out over the rasping, frozen roads. '"First to the right"' —must be this—second to the left, must be this—and there were the black gates. He got out, swung them open, and drove cautiously up a narrow, twisting drive, his headlights peering suspiciously round the bends. Those hedges wanted clipping, he thought, and this lane would have to be re-metalled—full of holes. Nasty drive up on a bad night; would cost some money, though.

The car began to climb steeply and swing to the right, and

presently the high hedges ended abruptly, and Mr Cort pulled up in front of Lorn Manor. He got out of the car, rubbed his hands, stamped his feet, and looked about him.

Lorn Manor was embedded half-way up a Chiltern spur and, as the agent had observed, 'commanded extensive vistas'. The place looked its age, Mr Cort decided, or rather ages, for the double Georgian brick chimneys warred with the Queen Anne left front. He could just make out the date, 1703, at the base of the nearest chimney. All that wing must have been added later. 'Big place, marvellous bargain at seven thousand; can't understand it. How those windows with their little curved eyebrows seem to frown down on one!' And then he turned and examined the 'vistas'. The trees were tinted exquisitely to an uncertain glory as the great red sinking sun flashed its rays on their crystal mantle. The vale of Aylesbury was drowsing beneath a slowly deepening shroud of mist. Above it the hills, their crests rounded and shaded by silver and rose coppices, seemed to have set in them great smoky eyes of flame where the last rays burned in them.

'It is like some dream world,' thought Mr Cort. 'It is curious how, wherever the sun strikes it seems to make an eye, and each one fixed on me; those hills, even those windows. But, judging from that mist, I shall have a slow journey home; I'd better have a quick look inside, though I have already taken a prejudice against the place—I hardly know why. Too lonely and isolated, perhaps.' And then the eyes blinked and closed, and it was dark.

He took a key from his pocket and went up three steps and thrust it into the key-hole of the massive oak door. The next moment he looked forward into absolute blackness, and the door swung to and closed behind him. This, of course, must be the 'palatial panelled hall' which the agent described. He must strike a match and find the light-switch. He fumbled in his pockets without success, and then he went through them again. He thought for a moment. 'I must have left them on the seat in the car,' he decided. 'I'll go and fetch them. The door must be just behind me here.'

He turned and groped his way back, and then drew himself up sharply, for it had seemed that something had slipped past him, and then he put out his hands—to touch the back of a chair, brocaded, he judged. He moved to the left of it and walked into a wall, changed his direction, went back past the chair, and found the wall again. He went back to the chair, sat down, and went through his pockets again, more thoroughly and carefully this time.

Well, there was nothing to get fussed about; he was bound to find the door sooner or later. Now, let him think. When he came in he had gone straight forward, three yards perhaps; but he couldn't have gone straight back, because he'd stumbled into this chair. The door must be a little to the left or the right of it. He'd try each in turn. He turned to the left first, and found himself going down a little narrow passage; he could feel its sides when he stretched out his hands. Well, then, he'd try the right. He did so, and walked into a wall. He groped his way along it, and again it seemed as if something slipped past him. 'I wonder if there's a bat in here?' he asked himself, and then found himself back at the chair.

How Rachel would laugh if she could see him now. Surely he had a stray match somewhere. He took off his overcoat and ran his hands round the seam of every pocket, and then he did the same to the coat and waistcoat of his suit. And then he put them on again. Well, he'd try again. He'd follow the wall along. He did so, and found himself in a little narrow passage. Suddenly he shot out his right hand, for he had the impression that something had brushed his face very lightly.

'I'm beginning to get a little bored with that bat, and with this blasted room generally,' he said to himself. 'I could imagine a more nervous person than myself getting a little fussed and panicky; but that's the one thing not to do.' Ah, here was that chair again. 'Now, I'll try the wall the other side.' Well, that seemed to go on for ever, so he retraced his steps till he found the chair, and sat down again. He whistled a little snatch resignedly. What an echo! The little tune had been flung back at him so fiercely, almost menacingly. Menacingly: that was just the feeble, panicky word a nervous person would use. Well, he'd go to the left again this time.

As he got up, a quick spurt of cold air fanned his face. 'Is anyone there?' he said. He had purposely not raised his voice—there was no need to shout. Of course, no one answered. Who could there have been to answer, since the caretaker was away? Now let him think it out. When he came in he must have gone straight forward and then swerved slightly on the way back; therefore—no, he was getting confused. At that moment he heard the whistle of a train, and felt reassured. The line from Wendover to Aylesbury ran half-left from the front door, so it should be about there—he pointed with his finger, got up, groped his way forward, and found himself in a little narrow passage. Well, he must turn back and go to the right this time. He did so, and something seemed to slip just past him, and then he scratched his finger slightly on the brocade of the chair.

'Talk about a maze,' he thought to himself; 'it's nothing to this.' And then he said to himself, under his breath: 'Curse this vile, god-forsaken place!' A silly, panicky thing to do he realized—almost as bad as shouting aloud. Well, it was obviously no use trying to find the door, he *couldn't* find it—*couldn't*. He'd sit in the chair till the light came. He sat down.

How very silent it was; his hands began searching in his pockets once more. Except for that sort of whispering sound over on the left somewhere—except for that, it was absolutely silent—except for that. What could it be? The caretaker was away. He turned his head slightly and listened intently. It was almost as if there were several people whispering together. One got curious sounds in old houses. How absurd it was! The chair couldn't be more than three or four yards from the door. There was no doubt about that. It must be slightly to one side or the other. He'd try the left once more. He got up, and something lightly brushed his face.

'Is anyone there?' he said, and this time he knew he had shouted. 'Who touched me? Who's whispering? Where's the door?' What a nervous fool he was to shout like that; yet someone outside might have heard him. He went groping forward again, and touched a wall. He followed along it, touching it with his finger-tips, and there was an opening.

The door, the door, it must be! And he found himself going down a little narrow passage. He turned and ran back. And then he remembered! He had put a match-booklet in his note-case! What a fool to have forgotten it, and made such an exhibition of himself. Yes, there it was; but his hands were trembling, and the booklet slipped through his fingers. He fell to his knees, and began searching about on the floor.

'It must be just here, it can't be far'—and then something icy-cold and damp was pressed against his forehead. He flung himself forward to seize it, but there was nothing there. And then he leapt to his feet, and with tears streaming down his face, cried: 'Who is there? Save me! Save me!' And then he began to run round and round, his arms outstretched. At last he stumbled against something, the chair—and something touched him as it slipped past. And then he ran screaming round the room; and suddenly his screams slashed back at him, for he was in a little narrow passage.

'Now, Mr Runt,' said the coroner, 'you say you heard screaming coming from the direction of the manor. Why didn't you go to find out what was the matter?'

'None of us chaps goes to manor after sundown,' said Mr Runt.

'Oh, I know there's some absurd superstition about the house; but you haven't answered the question. There were screams, obviously coming from someone who wanted help. Why didn't you go to see what was the matter, instead of running away?'

'None of us chaps goes to manor after sundown,' said Mr Runt.

'Don't fence with the question. Let me remind you that the doctor said Mr Cort must have had a seizure of some kind, but that had help been quickly forthcoming, his life might have been saved. Do you mean to tell me that, even if you had known this, you would still have acted in so cowardly a way?'

Mr Runt fixed his eyes on the ground and fingered his cap.

'None of us chaps goes to manor after sundown,' he repeated.

The Tibetan Box

ELIZABETH WALTER

It was during tea that the Tibetan box was first mentioned. As soon as she noticed it, incongruously perched on the rosewood work-table in the window, Alice Norrington wondered how she could possibly have overlooked it till then. In the same instant she asked in her most authoritarian manner, 'Mary, where did you get that box?'

From her sofa Mary Norrington followed the direction of her sister's gaze. She was not yet used to being a semi-invalid, and the excitement of her only sister's return after a three-year tour of duty in the mission field had tired her more than she wanted to admit. As if that were not enough, there was the strain of a third person's presence. She had somehow never suspected that her sister would be accompanied by her friend and colleague Ellen Whittaker. Equally, it had obviously never occurred to Alice that Miss Whittaker was not included in the invitation. An extra room had had to be made ready as unobtrusively as possible. Mrs Forrest, who 'did', had not been pleased. Moreover, since the moment of her arrival Alice had kept up a ceaseless catechism on Mary's health, finances, future plans, and wishes. Now she had started on the box.

'I bought it in a jumble sale,' Mary said tiredly. 'It's rather unusual, isn't it?'

'It's unusual to find anything worth buying in a jumble sale,' Miss Whittaker observed.

Alice was already on her feet. 'May I look at it?' she asked, moving briskly across the room at a rate that Mary now envied, remembering that she could have equalled it a mere six months ago. A moment later she was calling from the window: 'I say! This is magnificent. Ellen, come here and have a look at this.'

'Why don't you bring it nearer the fire?' Miss Whittaker asked placidly, continuing to sip her tea. The visit to Alice's sister was proving even more difficult than she had expected, and she had never expected very much. She had expressed her doubts about accompanying Alice, but Alice in her autocratic way had insisted that she should, and since Miss Whittaker had no friends or relatives in England, she had allowed her scruples to be overborne. Now, of course, she was regretting it. Her presence was too obviously neither anticipated nor desired. Moreover, as is often the way with sisters, Mary and Alice were too much alike to get on. The same imprudence, arrogance, and self-confidence—a 'strong personality', in short—were evident in both the Misses Norrington. They had never forgotten that they were the squire's daughters, and that it was for them to be liberal with advice, lofty in example, and inalienably right at all times. Alice, at least, possessed considerable administrative ability; the African mission field was pock-marked by her vigorous descents upon it; but neither sister possessed what Miss Whittaker would have described as humility. Mary, for all her weakened state, was the less humble of the two.

She was sitting up now with something of her old decisive manner. It was all very well for Alice to invade her home, even though that home was no more than four-bedroomed Throstle Cottage when once they had been used to living at The Hall. Times (and servants) might not be what they had been; incomes remain fixed in a world where all else rose; but an Englishwoman's home was still her castle and only one woman was in control.

'Bring the box over here, Alice,' she commanded, superimposing her orders on Miss Whittaker's request. 'And please draw the curtains while you're at the window. It's already beginning to get dark.'

She was right. The garden was filling with shadows. The trees, still in leaf for it was only October as yet, were bowing to one another in a gently rising wind. This will bring the leaves down, Alice Norrington reflected. We must sweep the garden and have a bonfire soon.

As though she had communicated her thoughts in some way, Mary said: 'We need another log on this fire, Alice dear. I wonder if you would be good enough to put one on.'

Her sister complied with some annoyance, placing the box on her chair. Mary's severe heart attack had in no way softened that organ. She was as autocratic as she had ever been. More so, in fact, for her invalid state gave her certain rights and privileges which she was not slow to abuse. Nevertheless, it seemed odd and unnatural to see Mary so much shrunken and aged. Her face had a greyness, despite a discreet use of make-up; the excitement of their arrival had made her pant. The doctor said bluntly it had been touch and go with her. It was doubtful if she would ever lead a normally active life again. And the attack had come without the slightest sign or warning. Since childhood, Mary had never had a day's illness in her life. If it came to that, Alice thought, she hadn't either. The Norringtons were what one might call healthy stock.

She smiled grimly and stood up, brushing her tweed skirt as she did so. Ellen Whittaker had picked up the box. It was on her lap, and from where she stood Alice could see it clearly. It reaffirmed her impression that it was a magnificent piece of work. Made of some unknown dark hardwood, its carvings burnished by age and care to a subtle sheen, it measured some 13 by 9 by 4 inches, and was fitted with a hinged lid and a lock. The key was missing, but this could hardly count as a defect, and the lid and sides of the box were so ornately and intricately carved that it would have been well worth snapping up at a jumble sale even if it had been in far worse condition. But who ever would give a box like that to a jumble sale?

'Major Murphy,' Mary said when asked, adding: 'I don't think you would know him, Alice. They only came here since you were last home on leave. They took the Red House on a seven-year renewable tenancy. We all liked them so much. Stella Murphy was a great gardener; she had that garden looking lovely. Such a pity the new people have let it go.'

'New people? Didn't the Murphys finish their tenancy?'

'My dear, the most dreadful thing! Stella died.'

'Good gracious,' Alice exclaimed, 'how tragic!'

'Tragic it certainly was. She jabbed the fork into her finger while bedding out some rock-plants. Such a little cut it was—I saw it. Within forty-eight hours she was dead. Tetanus. I never heard anything so dreadful.'

Alice duly echoed her sister, but Ellen Whittaker, who had seen and heard many dreadful things, did not. Instead, she asked, examining the box intently: 'Did the major tell you where this came from?'

'I don't think he knew,' Mary said. 'It actually belonged to Stella. I thought it rather unfeeling, putting something of hers in the sale. But perhaps he only wanted to help the church—he was leaving the district—and it was such an obvious snip. I asked him what he estimated it was worth and he said he thought a pound would be plenty. So I put in thirty shillings and took it home myself. I never thought to ask him where it came from, but it looks Chinese to me.'

Miss Whittaker shook her head decidedly. 'It's not Chinese. I can tell you that for sure. I'd say it was Tibetan.'

The sisters looked at her enquiringly. 'Ellen, how do you know?' Alice asked.

'I was in India before I came to Africa,' Miss Whittaker answered. 'I spent some time in Nepal. It's on the Tibetan border. I've seen a good deal of Tibetan work.'

'If you can read their writing,' Mary suggested, 'there's an inscription underneath that might help. I asked Major Murphy about it and he said he didn't know what it meant. I'm sure he was lying, somehow. It's probably something not quite nice.'

'The carvings don't look particularly erotic,' Alice observed with interest. 'Offhand, I'd have said they were threatening in some way.'

The adjective was a disturbingly apt one. The surface of the lid was filled by a rampant dragon, his face surrounded by a curious beard or frill. His eyes must originally have been jewels, but now only the empty sockets remained. From these flared two long whiskers, like a mandarin's moustache. Face and body were covered with fish-like scales, and a ridge of spines ran down the centre of the back. One fore-foot was raised as if to lash out, and every foot had four wicked-looking claws. The body writhed and coiled in undulation, this way and that across the lid. The tail, with a final upward flick towards the vertical, was finished with a vicious little barb. Round the sides of the box were lesser dragons, carved in profile but equally aroused. Two dragons faced each other on the long side; on the short, a single dragon glared outwards at the world.

'There seems no reason why the major shouldn't have translated the inscription,' Alice continued. 'Do you think he knew what it said?'

'He very well may have done. I understand he was in the Indian Army.'

'And how long ago did all this take place?' Alice questioned.

'It's seven months today since I bought the box,' Mary said. Seeing her sister look startled, she elaborated. 'The jumble sale was on a Saturday. Contributions were brought in on Thursday to leave us Friday for marking and pricing the stuff. So I bought the box on a Thursday, and three weeks later I had my heart attack. I remember when that was without trying, so that makes it seven months to the day. It's a pity there wasn't a longer interval,' she added. 'I was going to have the dragon's missing eyes restored. I thought rubies, perhaps—very small and deep and glowing.'

She was interrupted by a cry from Ellen Whittaker, who was gazing intently at the underside of the box.

'What is it?' Alice asked. 'A protruding nail?'

'No, oh no. It's nothing like that. It's this . . . this inscription.'

'Do you mean to say you can read it?'

'I'm afraid I can.'

Mary clapped her hands in childlike triumph. 'I'm so glad. I've been longing to know what it says.'

'You won't be so glad when you hear it.'

'Is it really something obscene?'

'I wish it were,' Ellen Whittaker said grimly. She put the box on the floor and drew imperceptibly away. 'It's Tibetan all right,' she informed them. 'A Tibetan magician's box. In it would have been kept all the tools of his art or profession, closely guarded from curious eyes.'

'A sort of conjuror's box,' Alice suggested.

'No, something more sinister than that. There is no accounting for the power of these magicians. No rational explanation will suffice. They can bless or curse with equal efficaciousness, and the inscription on the box is a curse.'

'What a terrible hold superstition has on these people!' Alice Norrington was already planning a crusade.

Miss Whittaker answered her sharply. 'Superstition's hardly the word. You don't have to believe in their magic to be affected.'

'Even in England?' Mary enquired.

Miss Whittaker did not trouble to answer. She had seen Tibetan magic at work. But the Misses Norrington, younger and less experienced, were clamorous to know details.

'Why the curse?' Alice Norrington demanded.

'In case the box was stolen,' her friend replied. 'The magician's is a hereditary calling. The box would be handed down from father to son. It could only fall into unauthorized hands because it was stolen—in the first instance, at any rate. Hence the curse on all those who possess it. They have no right to it, you see.'

'I like that!' Mary Norrington exclaimed angrily. 'I paid a perfectly fair price for that box.' Her anger was the greater because it was not strictly ethical to buy items before the jumble sale had started. She remembered Major Murphy had looked at her oddly at the time. 'There was nothing dishonest about my acquiring it,' she said defensively.

'How did Major Murphy get hold of it, do you know?'

'I told you, it belonged to Stella.'

'The woman who died of tetanus. Ah yes.'

Miss Whittaker stood up abruptly, clasping her hands behind her, feet astride. She looked oddly out of place among the chintz and afternoon tea-things of Throstle Cottage—too gaunt, too sallow, too much an archetype. 'Mary,' she announced, putting all the urgency into her words of which she was capable, 'you must get rid of that accursed box.'

'Certainly not. It's one of my favourite possessions.'

'If you don't, you'll be dead in six months.'

'Whatever are you talking about, Ellen? What has the box to do with me?'

'Merely that it promises death within a twelvemonth to all unlawful possessors. You've already had half your time.'

There was a moment's horrified silence. Then Mary Norrington gave a shaky laugh. 'You're not going to tell me you believe this nonsense, Ellen? You, a worker in the Christian mission field!'

'Christianity has nothing to do with it,' Miss Whittaker answered firmly. 'These magicians have a curious control over natural forces, to which the human body is as much subject as anything else. I needn't point out the coincidence of your having a heart attack three weeks after you first acquired the box. I beg you to get rid of it before further mischief comes upon you—as most assuredly it will.'

Her sincerity was so obvious that Mary Norrington began to hesitate. The heart attack that had so sorely reduced her had come like a bolt from the blue. There was no history of cardiac disorder in the family, and she herself had seemed as strong as an ox. Her doctor had been quite unable to account for it, although he assured her there was nothing unique about her case. What was even more disturbing was her failure to make a good recovery. Six months later she was still as weak as a kitten, and this had been preying on her mind.

None the less, she had no intention of yielding to Ellen Whittaker's superstition. Such a show of respect for heathen practice should receive no condonation from her.

'I hardly see how I can give the box away,' she said sweetly, 'now that you have acquainted me with the nature of the curse. It would be tantamount, surely, to murder. I do not think I could bring myself to commit that.'

'The best thing would be to return it to Tibet,' Miss Whittaker suggested, 'and hope that it falls into good hands.'

'There might be difficulties with the Customs declaration. Besides, can one send things to Tibet?'

'I have a friend in India who might help us.'

'Why go to so much trouble?' Alice Norrington asked. She had been listening uneasily to the argument, which reflected her own divided state of mind. On the one hand, her faith and reason were against it; on the other, was the fact that Mary was ill. And there was not only Mary, but also the previous owner, the late Mrs Murphy. Of course, both could be coincidence merely. All the same, it was unpleasantly odd.

But Alice's was a direct, uncomplicated nature. The devious was foreign to her mind. She was accustomed to going to the root of any problem, and her solutions were effective, if extreme. 'Why bother to return the box to Tibet?' she repeated. 'Why not simply destroy it here and now?'

Mary smiled at her with sisterly approval. 'An excellent notion, my dear.'

With Alice, thought was quickly succeeded by action. 'If you have no objection, I will attend to it straightaway. There is no doubt a hatchet in the cellar. I will chop it up for firewood at once.'

'I wouldn't, if I were you, Alice.' Miss Whittaker had gone very pale.

Both sisters regarded her in amazement. 'Ellen, what is it? Are you ill?'

'No, no. But you must not touch that box. It is dangerous.'

'I really must ask you to explain.'

'There is another line in the inscription,' Miss Whittaker whispered. 'It promises destruction to anyone attempting to destroy.'

'So one can neither keep the box nor destroy it. What can one do with it, may I ask?'

Miss Whittaker shook her head helplessly. 'You can only send it back.'

'Nonsense, Ellen.' Alice Norrington spoke very firmly. 'You must not allow these superstitious thoughts to get a hold. You will soon be little better than the heathen you are supposed to be converting. This error must be rooted out at once. I shall go to the cellar now and dispose of this ridiculous Tibetan magic box for ever. No—'as her friend put out a restraining hand— 'don't try to stop me. I have quite made up my mind.'

'You will regret it,' Ellen Whittaker murmured. 'You will regret it all your life, or what is left.'

Alice Norrington did not bother to answer, and a moment later they heard her going down the cellar stairs. The cellar was directly under the sitting-room, and they could hear her moving about, shifting the chopping-block into position and then a clatter as she dropped the axe. Mary Norrington jumped as though the blade had bitten into her, but Miss Whittaker showed all the calmness of despair. A moment later they heard the first ringing blows of the hatchet, and perceptibly they both relaxed.

'When one is ill,' Mary said apologetically, 'one so easily becomes overwrought.'

'When one has spent long years on the Tibetan border,' Miss Whittaker responded bravely, 'one forgets that in England its standards do not apply.'

Before she had finished speaking, both women were paralysed by a hoarse and terrible cry. It rose out of the depths of the cellarage beneath them, an animal cry of anguish and pain and fear. The voice was recognizably Alice Norrington's. A moment later they heard her stumbling up the stairs.

Both listeners were on their feet in an instant, but Miss Whittaker was first through the door. The cellar door opened into the hall of Throstle Cottage. Alice Norrington had almost reached the top of the cellar stairs. She had been silent since that first inexplicable scream of terror, but they could hear the rasping of her breath. Mary was leaning, white-faced, upon the hall table. It fell to Miss Whittaker to move towards the cellar door.

She was half-way across the hall when Alice entered. Her features were still rigid from the shock she had undergone, blood was spurting from a hand on which three fingers were now missing, her protruding eyes were fixed unseeingly in space.

Mary hid her face in her hands with a little cry of horror, but it was not the first time Ellen Whittaker had faced emergency. She had seen violent death and bodies torn and broken, and her common sense and energy, as usual, did not fail to respond. Almost before her senses had recovered, her brain was active, propelling her body forwards, uttering commands.

'It's all right, Alice, don't be frightened. Mary, the doctor— quick! No, give me the table-napkins before you telephone. We'll use them as pressure pads. Keep your head down, Alice, it may help you to feel better. I promise you, we'll not let you die of this.'

Half carrying, half dragging, she got the fainting Alice to a chair. Mary was already dialling the doctor's number as she applied pressure to the artery in the wrist. To her relief, the blood-spurts slackened and slowed to nothing, although the blood continued to well out copiously. Alice moaned and stirred and endeavoured to sit upright.

'It's all right,' Miss Whittaker reassured her. 'It's better you shouldn't look.'

Alice took no notice of the injunction. Her eyes were still staring and wild. From the sitting-room Mary's voice on the telephone came faintly: '. . . my sister . . . an accident . . . come at once . . .'

Suddenly Alice gripped her friend's arm with unexpected intensity. Her fingertips were cold on Miss Whittaker's flesh.

'It was the box,' she whispered hoarsely. 'It moved as I was about to strike it and dragged my fingers under the axe. Otherwise it would never have happened. But the box moved and I couldn't stop it. I tell you, Ellen, the Tibetan box moved!'

While Alice Norrington was in hospital, Miss Whittaker remained at Throstle Cottage in a position which she rapidly recognized as that of unpaid companion-drudge. There was no doubt that Mary Norrington had been shaken by her sister's accident. There was equally no doubt that with her heart condition shock and distress were liable to bring on another attack, which attack might possibly prove fatal; but this was problematical. Miss Whittaker could not feel that it warranted the day-in, day-out attendance she was obviously expected to provide. By the end of the first week she had had enough not only of Mary's tyranny, but of Mary's patronage, which was worse.

It began with Miss Whittaker's appearance. Mary had no scruples about making personal remarks. Indeed, it amused Miss Whittaker to note the resemblance between the sisters, except that, whereas Alice spent her energies in the mission field, Mary Norrington pursued lesser ends nearer home. But she adopted the same bludgeoning tactics as her sister, with possibly comparable results, for while there was no doubt that Alice was effective in securing conversions, Miss Whittaker wondered to what extent they represented change of heart. She was half amused, half horrified to find herself giving way to Mary, putting cold cream on her face for the first time in twenty years, and treating her dry hair to an oil bath before a special shampoo. She consoled herself that she was doing it for Alice, but she was too honest to accept such glazing for long. She was doing it for the sake of peace and quietness. Alice's converts presumably did the same.

The thought of Alice as a colleague brought back to her the tragic aspect of the affair, for with her maimed hand it seemed unlikely that Alice would ever be passed fit for service in the mission field again. Moreover, her nervous system had suffered a severe shock, and the tense, fevered woman who laid her sound hand like a claw on Miss Whittaker's arm whenever they were alone together and besought her to get rid of the Tibetan box was someone very different from the active, no-nonsense colleague whom Ellen Whittaker had always known. By common consent they did not mention the matter to Mary, who knew nothing of her sister's allegation about the box.

Mary tended, indeed, to dismiss the element of superstition in the accident. 'Alice has always considered herself too practical,' she claimed. 'It was inevitable that she should some day have to recognize her limitations. Why, she could not even thinly slice a loaf of bread! To attempt to chop up hardwood was sheer folly.'

Miss Whittaker thought she did not exaggerate, though of course it had not been Mary who had had to venture into the cellar, blood-bespattered like a slaughter-house, and retrieve the box to which Alice Norrington's fingers were adhering, glued into place by sticky, congealing blood. If it had been, Miss Whittaker thought grimly, she could not have borne to restore the box to its accustomed place in the sitting-room, where its incongruous presence was now emphasized by a gash from the axe along the edge of the lid. She wondered if Mary would be insensitive enough to leave the box there when her sister came out of hospital. She was rather afraid that she would.

Her surprise and relief were therefore considerable when, returning from a visit to Alice one afternoon, she saw that the box had gone from the rosewood work-table in the window. Before she could enquire the reason, Mrs Forrest came in to say that Miss Mary was lying down in her room.

'Is she worse?' Miss Whittaker demanded, fearing some fresh disaster.

'The vicar called and then she was took poorly. She said I was to ask you to go in.'

The vicar's visits were not usually distressing. Miss Whittaker hastened to ascertain the facts. Tapping at the door of the bedroom (the former dining-room, since Mary was now unable to manage stairs), she found her sitting up in bed with the same tense and twitching anxiety that her injured sister habitually displayed.

'What's the matter?' Miss Whittaker asked non-committally.

'I have had a very serious shock. It means that you are right about the box, Ellen. We must certainly dispose of it at once.'

Miss Whittaker wondered what the vicar could have had to do with this development. She was not left long in doubt.

'We had been speaking of Alice's accident,' Mary Norrington said faintly, 'and I remembered what you said about the box—how it must have been stolen in the first place because such objects were always handed down. It occurred to me to ask the vicar if he had any idea how Stella had acquired it, and to my surprise he had. He said she inherited it from her father only six months before she died.'

'An old family treasure?' Miss Whittaker enquired softly, though the sinking of her heart already told her this was not going to prove to be the case.

'Not at all. The old man had bought it at an auction without even knowing what it was. He was something of an antique collector, and had bid for a mahogany roll-top desk. When the desk was delivered, the box was discovered in a drawer. The auctioneer said he could reckon it as part of the lot. He had no interest in it and stored it away in an attic, where it was found only after his death. Because he too died, Ellen, within a year of acquiring it. He caught pneumonia and it proved too much for his heart. So it begins to look as if you're right about the curse, doesn't it? Especially when I tell you this last bit.'

'You remember I told you Stella's father bought the box accidentally at an auction? Well, do you know why that auction was taking place?'

'I can guess,' Miss Whittaker murmured *sotto voce*. Mary Norrington seemed not to hear.

'The owner of the house had been killed in a car crash,' she whispered. 'His widow put everything up for sale. I don't know how long he'd had the box or who'd had it before him, but I am certain the box was to blame. So many deaths cannot be coincidence. I was foolish not to have believed you before. There is clearly something noxious about the object. I have had Mrs Forrest put it in the garden shed.'

'That won't save you,' Miss Whittaker said automatically.

Mary Norrington gripped her arm. 'Then what will? We cannot give it away because it will bring destruction upon others, and we know what happened when Alice tried to chop it up. Of course she is, as I say, rather clumsy, but I should not wish anyone else to try. How, then, are we to rid ourselves of this evil object? Or must I, like its previous owners, die?'

'We could burn it,' Miss Whittaker said slowly. 'Magic is supposed to have no power against fire.'

'Like burning a witch in the old days?'

'Yes,' Ellen Whittaker answered. 'A little like that.'

'And would you be prepared to burn it? Do you think it would be safe for you to try?'

Miss Whittaker looked thoughtful. 'Yes, I think so. At any rate, I am prepared to make the attempt. Only not in the house—in the garden. I will do it tomorrow if it is fine.'

Mary Norrington relaxed against her pillows. 'Dear Ellen, what should I do without you? You are such a tower of strength. And I believe your hair is looking better for that oil treatment. We must remember to try another one quite soon.'

Miss Whittaker was for once glad to take up the subject of her appearance in preference to the burning of the box. She was reluctant to admit to Mary Norrington that her knowledge of magic was greater than she had disclosed. For Ellen Whittaker was intellectually adventurous, and by no means prepared to stop short at the limits of Christian belief when there was something outside it that seemed worth her exploration. In Nepal she had made friends with a magician, who, besides much else, had taught her a secret sign, which would, he claimed, protect her from all danger should anyone ever lay a spell on her. Miss Whittaker had been suitably grateful, having witnessed Tibetan magic at work, but she had shortly afterwards been posted to Africa and had never needed to make use of the sign. She was relieved about this for several different reasons, not the least being that she felt it incompatible with her faith. To enquire into native magic was one thing; to resort to its ritual, something else. For this reason she had never mentioned her knowledge; in fact, she had half forgotten it herself, until the destruction of the Tibetan box became imperative and she realized that the task must fall to her. For she alone had the power to overcome its magic, provided she used the chosen agent, fire.

The next day was fine and almost windless. Miss Whittaker resolved to have her bonfire after lunch. The morning was spent in preparation, for she was anxious that nothing should go wrong. She had amassed a pile of leaves and withered branches, chrysanthemum stalks and rotting flower-heads, and to these she added firewood from the cellar, old newspapers, and a paraffin-impregnated briquette. The pyre was built at the very bottom of the garden, on waste ground sheltered by the angle of the wall which at this point was bare of fruit trees, so that no living thing should suffer any harm.

Nevertheless, Miss Whittaker knew a certain uneasiness which common sense was unable to dispel. Perhaps it was this that made her place two buckets of water within easy reach of her prospective blaze. She was taking no chances with magic, and that included her own untried magic power. She was relieved when Mary Norrington announced that she would not be present at the incineration; she would not even watch from the sitting-room. This meant that there would be no one to witness the operation, for the nearest house was some little distance away. Mrs Forrest went home at two-thirty. Whatever happened, there would be no one there to see. If it became necessary to resort to the use of magic, Miss Whittaker could do so in secret and alone.

All the same, she sincerely hoped it would not be necessary and took all scientific precautions first. In addition to the two buckets of water, she equipped herself with tongs and a rake. Stout shoes and thick socks protected feet and ankles, and her hands were shielded by heavy gauntlet gloves. Her tweed skirt would have smothered fire sooner than kindle; the same went for her cardigan of Shetland wool. Her head was muffled in a scarf tied turban-fashion; not a single lock poked forth from underneath. Miss Whittaker was particularly careful with the turban, which was doing double duty that afternoon. Not only did it serve to protect her hair from ash-fragments, but it also concealed its unappetisingly greasy state, Miss Whittaker having submitted that morning to another of Mary Norrington's oil treatments, to be followed that evening by another special shampoo.

But between the morning and the evening came the afternoon, and Mary had retired for her rest. Clutching the box to her like a living creature, Miss Whittaker made a conspiratorial exit from the garden shed. The sun was shining with almost the warmth of summer. She felt herself sweating under her wool and tweed. The thought of fire-heat as well was intolerable. She had a sudden impulse to go back. The sharp contours of the box recalled her to a sense of duty. To leave it intact would mean that Mary Norrington must die; or if not Mary, some other innocent possessor. There was nothing for it; the box must be destroyed. And the burning of wood was an entirely natural process. There was no reason why she should feel this growing fear. Besides, if the worst happened and there were unnatural manifestations, she had only to make the sign. The magician had assured her it was infallible; whatsoever saw it must withdraw at once. She was probably the one person in England who could burn the box in safety. With trembling hands, she knelt and lighted the pyre.

The paraffin briquette caught at once and so did the paper; then the sticks kindled into a lively blaze. The twigs caught, and some of the drier dead leaves crackled. The smell of autumn burning filled the air. The bonfire was built high in the centre to support a level platform of sticks. Miss Whittaker approached and placed the Tibetan box upon it, then stepped backwards with a nervous little gasp.

The fire continued to burn brightly, with much crackling and showering of sparks. Then, as it spread to the damp leaves, stalks and flower-heads, it began to give off smoke. Miss Whittaker drew back, coughing. She had not supposed there would be so pungent a smell. The fire, too, was burning less brightly. The afternoon seemed suddenly overcast. Looking up, she was astonished to see the smoke reeling in dense black clouds overhead, forming a tented ceiling above her, shutting out the sky and the sun. Meanwhile, its columns continued to wreathe upwards with a curious serpentine twine, so black they appeared to have substance and to move in response to some directional control.

The box had remained untouched in the centre of the bonfire, which was subsiding now into ash. So far as Miss Whittaker could see, the flames had not even touched it. She poked nervously with the rake, causing the platform of sticks to collapse with a sputter, tilting the box on to its side. The smoke was growing momently more acrid. It was becoming difficult to breathe. Miss Whittaker's eyes were watering. She clapped a handkerchief to her nose.

No doubt it was blurred vision that first made her perceive in the smoke-coils a vaguely remembered design. That double curve folding back on itself with a foot uplifted—was it not the dragon of the box? She wiped her eyes, blaming an over-strained nervous system, and looked again. But surely those were scales! Black and sinuous and almost stationary, the dragon reared up from the pyre. The terrible four-clawed feet were extended, groping. The head, in profile now, moved lightly from side to side. Miss Whittaker could see clearly the protective frill surrounding jaw and throat. The mandarin whiskers, even longer and thinner than she remembered them, trailed off into wisps of smoke. Now and again a puff exuded from the wide-spaced, flaring nostrils. Each time the cavernous mouth opened, there was a rolling belch of smoke.

The dragon seemed to be searching for something. Its body made sudden lurches in the air. It was for all the world as if it were playing blind man's buff with an imaginary opponent, who, fortunately for him, was never there. For there was no doubt of the dragon's hostile intentions. The groping claws were poised to seize and tear, and the size of the creature was such that a full-grown buffalo could have been dismembered as easily as a rat.

Miss Whittaker watched in horrified fascination. She had never seen anything to equal this. This was Tibetan magic with a vengeance—which was what the dragon appeared to desire. And she herself was its immediate object! Instinctively she drew a little further back. It was one thing to know the sign which would invalidate Tibetan magic, but quite another to have to put it into use. She flexed her fingers into the required position. At least she had not forgotten what to do. It was comforting to realize that she had power over this dragon, who looked so terrible and black.

A twig snapped sharply behind her. As if it had heard, the dragon turned its head. The long neck undulated gently. At the other end of the beast the barbed tail lashed. The smoke which composed the dragon had now completely blotted out the sky. The brightness of the flames had sunk to the dull glow of ashes. A wind seemed suddenly to have sprung up. It lifted the frill about the dragon's jaw-line. The mandarin whiskers streamed wide. The distended nostrils were a-quiver, as the dragon sought to scent its prey.

Suddenly the head poised in its veering peregrinations. Despite the smoke, it had caught Miss Whittaker's scent. With a tremendous writhe of all its coils and convolutions, it reared up to its full height. The claws were fully extended. Some four feet above her the bearded face looked down. It held an indescribable weight of menace. For all her confidence, Miss Whittaker began to be afraid. She raised her hand in the required ritual gesture, and looked up to meet the dragon's gaze. It peered down at her, evil and impassive, from the orbless sockets of its eyes.

With a little scream, Miss Whittaker flung herself sideways as the dragon's claws lashed down. They missed her, but she felt the wind of their passing. The dragon reared itself again. Now that it seemed to have her scent in its nostrils, it proved impossible for her to evade. Whichever way she darted in the smoke-pall, the blind monster's claws were just behind. There was a clatter as she knocked over the buckets. The water spread round her, soaking her socks and shoes. She was already exhausted and panting, the acrid fumes from the pyre were making her choke and cough. The house, the garden, seemed suddenly to have receded. There was only darkness and smoke.

On the fire which gave the dragon its being, the Tibetan box lay up-ended, still untouched. If only the flames would consume it, the dragon would surely cease to exist. Seizing the rake, Miss Whittaker made one last desperate assault upon it and thrust it into the heart of the fire, while the dragon reared

itself above her, preparing to nail her to the ground. At the last moment, by a dexterous twist and feint, she escaped it. A shower of sparks rained down. They smouldered for a moment on her heavy woollen garments. Gasping, Miss Whittaker beat them out.

One corner of the box had taken; the wood was beginning to char. The dragon, though still dangerous, appeared to be shrinking. The clouds of smoke were less voluminous, less dense. Yet the heat seemed all at once to have become quite insupportable. Miss Whittaker had a sudden glimpse of the sun. She saw the house, the garden, the chrysanthemums and the apple-trees, the peaceful normality of it all. Then, as an unquenched spark ignited her oil-soaked hair into combustion, she ran screaming towards the house.

She did not see her bonfire fall apart and burn itself out in isolated patches. She did not see the Tibetan box roll free. She saw only the horrified face of Mary Norrington, as she emerged from her room into the hall.

'Mary, help me! Help me!' Miss Whittaker screamed in terror, endeavouring to beat out the flames.

But Mary only stood white-faced and clutching the door-post, unable either to move or speak. She saw before her Ellen Whittaker's body, on her head a strange corona of flame, the skin of the scalp already blackening and peeling, the face distorted beyond belief. This apparition from Hell was advancing towards her. The Tibetan box's curse was coming true. With a cry, Mary Norrington doubled up in the doorway. She was dead before her body reached the ground.

The 'Double Tragedy at Throstle Cottage', as the newspapers called it, did nothing to reassure Miss Alice Norrington as to the innocuous nature of the box. Nor did her convictions regarding this fire- and axe-scarred object and her insistence on returning it (via the late Miss Whittaker's friend in India) to Tibet do anything to reassure her superiors at evangelical headquarters as to her suitability for return to the mission field. She was compulsorily retired from service (without too much protesting on her part) and now lives on the south coast near Worthing and attends psychometry readings once a week.

Momster in the Closet

JANE YOLEN

There's a momster in my closet,' Kenny said. 'I heard
him this morning.'

'Grumpf ouff,' Dad said, his mouth full.

'That's nice, dear. Do you want more?' Mom asked.

You see, with Kenny it was something new in that closet
every day. At five—'And a half!' he'd be quick to remind you—
he had more imagination than sense. Also, he watched too
much TV.

'Come on, squirt,' I said, 'or we'll be late.' I took an extra-
long swallow as Kenny shrugged into his backpack. He
followed me out the door.

'Was, too, a momster,' he said.

'Monster,' I corrected automatically.

'With long grungy hair. And weird claws. He was nine feet
. . . no, ten feet tall.'

'Heard all that through the door?' I asked.

That shut him up. Of course, last week it had been a weirdwolf. The time before it had been a ghould. He didn't know how to pronounce the stuff, but he was convinced they were all there. That must be *some* closet, I thought, and said so out loud.

'Right to Momster Land,' Kenny said.

Kids! I could hardly recall ever being that young. It felt as if I had been a teenager forever.

When we got home, the sun was sitting just below the horizon. Summers are hard around here. There is just not enough night.

'Come on, squirt,' I said. 'Time for bed.'

'I don't want to go,' Kenny said. 'There's a momster in the closet.'

'You have to. I have to. That's the way of the world,' I said. 'Besides, it's monster. Spelled with an *n* not an *m*.'

'It's got spells, too?' Kenny said. 'Oh, no—it will *really* get me.'

'There's nothing there,' I said, my patience beginning to go. 'Besides, if it threatens you, just growl back at it and show your teeth like this.' I bared my fangs at him.

Kenny giggled.

We went inside. Mom was already settled down, but Dad was still up, sitting in front of the TV and watching the flag flapping in time to the National Anthem. It's only a little more exciting than a test pattern. He didn't seem to hear us.

Kenny and I went into the room we shared, and I helped him get undressed. He still has trouble with the knots in his shoelaces. I keep asking Mom to find him a pair of Velcro sneakers.

Once we were in our pyjamas and had brushed our teeth, he raced ahead of me to his bed. He turned for a moment and growled at the closet.

'Fangs for the memory,' I said.

He giggled again, though I don't think he got the joke.

'Last one in is a . . .' he shouted.

'. . . rotten . . .' I prompted.

'. . . corpse!' He made a funny face and lay down. Once his eyes were closed, he was very still.

I kissed his forehead, moving aside the hair as white-gold as corn silk, and tenderly closed the lid over him. Then I climbed into my own coffin, pulling it shut before the first light of day could come streaming through the blinds. Monsters in the closet, indeed! Kenny knew, as I did, that only sunlight or a stake through the heart can really kill a vampire.

I closed my eyes and slept.

Acknowledgements

Marian Abbey: 'Moving House', © 1996 Marian Abbey, first published here by permission of the author. **Margot Arnold:** 'The Girl in the Mirror', first published in Mary Danby (ed*): The Eighth Armada Ghost Book* (Fontana, 1976), reprinted by permission of HarperCollins Publishers Ltd. **Ramsey Campbell:** 'Conversion', from *Dark Companions* (Fontana, 1982), reprinted by permission of HarperCollins Publishers Ltd. and The Carol Smith Literary Agency on behalf of the author. **Angela Carter:** 'The Werewolf', from *The Bloody Chamber and Other Stories* (Victor Gollancz, 1979), Copyright © The Estate of Angela Carter 1995, reproduced by permission of the Estate of Angela Carter, c/o Rogers, Coleridge & White Ltd., 20 Powis Mews, London W11 1JN. **Michael Chislett:** 'Goodman's Tenants', first published in Barbara and Christopher Roden (eds): *All Hallows 10*, October 1995, The Journal of the Ghost Story Society, reprinted by permission of the author. **Stephen Elboz:** 'Mother', © 1996 Stephen Elboz, first published here by permission of the author. **Adèle Geras:** 'Captain Ashe's Daughter', from *A Lane to the Land of the Dead* (Hamish Hamilton, 1994) © Adèle Geras 1994, reprinted by permission of Laura Cecil Literary Agency on behalf of the author. **John Gordon:** 'Bewitched', © 1996 John Gordon, first published here by permission of A. P. Watt Ltd. on behalf of the author. **Mick Gowar:** 'The Flying Dustman', © 1996 Mick Gowar, first published here by permission of the author. **Grace Hallworth:** 'The Intake', from *Mouth Open, Story Jump Out* by Grace Hallworth (Methuen Children's Books, 1984), reprinted by permission of Reed Books. **Dennis Hamley:** 'Dog On Board', © 1996 Dennis Hamley, first published here by permission of the author. **Brian Jacques:** 'Bridgey', from *Seven Strange and Ghostly Tales* by Brian Jacques (Hutchinson Children's Books, 1991), Copyright © 1991 by Brian Jacques, reprinted by permission of Random House UK Ltd. and Philomel Books. **M. R. James:** 'The Ash Tree', from *Ghost Stories of the Antiquary* (Arnold, 1904), reprinted by permission of N. J. R. James. **F. G. Loring:** 'The Tomb of Sarah', first published in *Pall Mall Magazine*, December 1990. **Philippa Pearce:** 'The Hirn', from *Who's Afraid? and Other Strange Stories* (Puffin), © 1986 Philippa Pearce, reprinted by permission of the author via Laura Cecil Literary Agency. **Alison Prince:** 'The Baby-sitter', from *Haunted Children* by Alison Prince (Methuen Children's Books, 1982), reprinted by permission of Reed Books. **Ralph Prince:** 'The Water Woman and Her Lover', first published in *BIM* (The Literary Magazine of Barbados), Vol.13 No. 53. **Garnett Radcliffe:** 'The Gloves', first published in *Weird Tales Magazine*, Copyright © 1953 by Weird Tales, reprinted by permission of Weird Tales Ltd. **Laurence Staig:** 'Do You Dance?' © 1996 Laurence Staig, first published here by permission of the author. **Terry Tapp:** 'The Junk Room', first published in Mary Danby (ed): *The Fourteenth Armada Ghost Book* (Fontana, 1982), reprinted by permission of HarperCollins Publishers Ltd. **H. Russell Wakefield:** 'Blind Man's Buff', originally published in *Old Man's Beard* (G. Bles, 1929), reprinted in Richard Dalby (ed): *The Best Ghost Stories of H. Russell Wakefield* (John Murray, 1978) reprinted with permission of the author's heirs. **Elizabeth Walter:** 'The Tibetan Box' from *Snowfall and Other Chilling Events* (The Harvill Press, London 1965), Copyright © Elizabeth Walter 1965, reprinted by permission of the author. **Jane Yolen:** 'Momster in the Closet', Copyright © 1993 by Jane Yolen, first published in *Bruce Colville's Book of Monsters* (Scholastic, Inc.), reprinted by permission of Curtis Brown, Ltd., New York.

While every effort has been made to trace and contact copyright holders this has not always been possible. If notified, the publisher will be pleased to rectify any errors or omissions at the earliest opportunity.

The illustrations are by:
Martin J. Cottam pp iii, 25, 31, 140, 147, 149, 157, 163, 193, 202, 211
Jonathon Heap pp 36, 66, 73, 77, 164, 170
Ian Miller pp 16, 20, 22, 52, 63, 70, 100, 105, 114, 129, 137, 175, 186, 213
Brian Pedley pp 1, 5, 41, 47, 88, 95, 115, 125, 188
Barry Wilkinson, B. L. Kearley Ltd. pp 7, 11, 83, 85, 150, 156

The original photography on the cover is by Rob Judges, the computer manipulation is by Slatter-Anderson.